The Greatest Guitar Songbook

W9-DIR-028

ISBN 978-0-634-00017-1

HAL•LEONARD® CORPORATION

7777 W. BLUEMOUND RD. P.O. BOX 13819 MILWAUKEE, WI 53213

Visit Hal Leonard Online at
www.halleonard.com

The Greatest Guitar Songbook

Chord Melody Guitar

Classical Guitar

Fingerstyle Guitar

Guitar Riffs

Blackbird

Words and Music by John Lennon and Paul McCartney

*Strum upstemmed notes w/ index fin. of pick hand whenever more than one upstemmed note appears.

1., 3. Black - bird sing - ing in the dead of night,
2. Black - bird sing - ing in the dead of night,

take___ these bro - ken wings ___ and learn ___ to fly. ___
take___ these sunk - en eyes ___ and learn ___ to see. ___

All your ___ life, ___

you were on - ly wait - ing for the mo -
you were on - ly wait - ing for the mo -

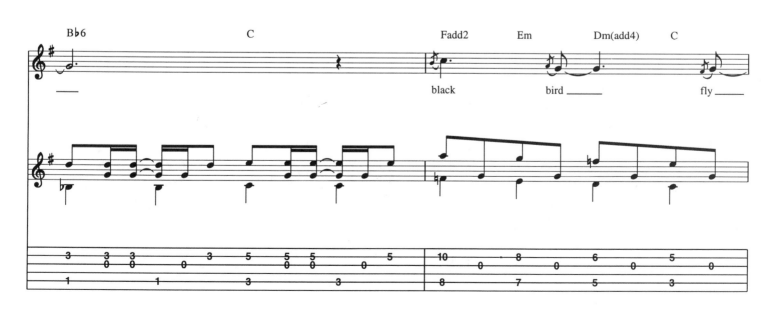

5

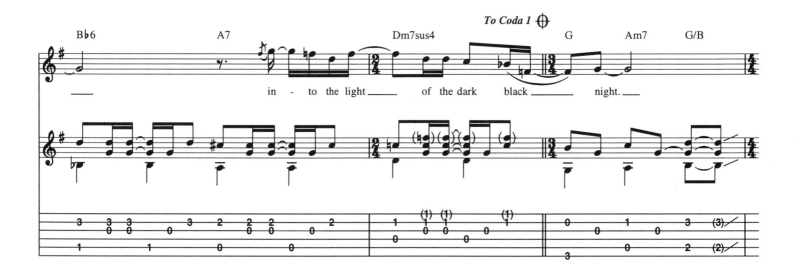

in - to the light ____ of the dark black ____ night. ____

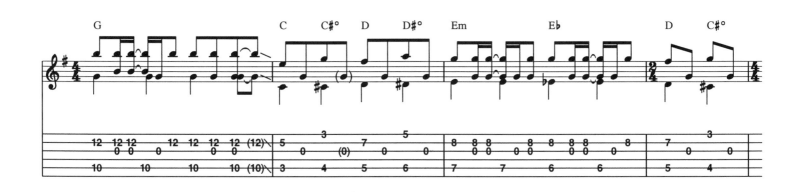

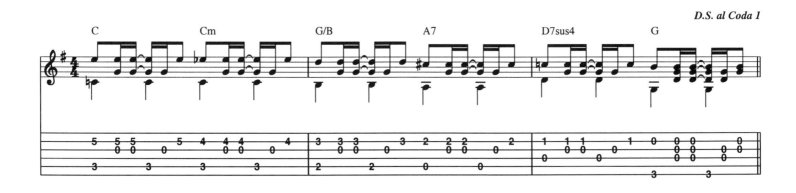

D.S. al Coda 1

⊕ Coda 1

____ night.

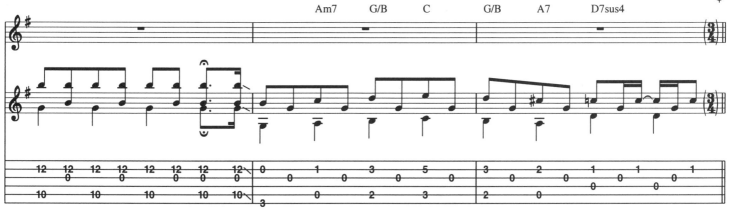

⊕ Coda 2

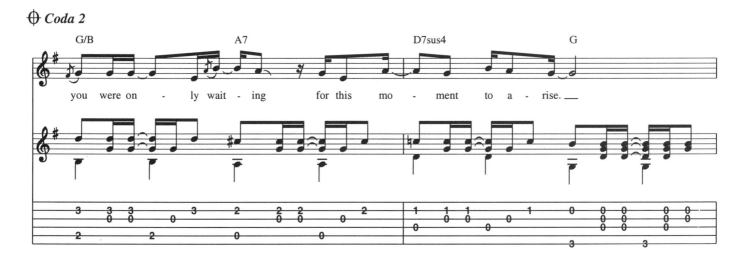

you were on - ly wait - ing for this mo - ment to a - rise. __

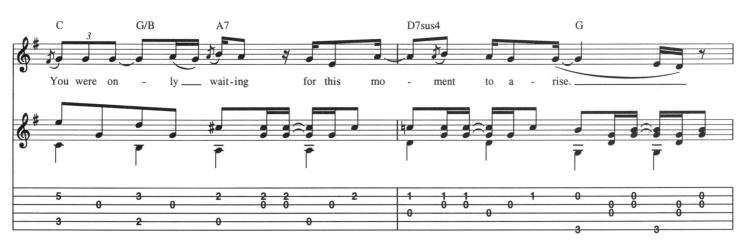

You were on - ly __ wait-ing for this mo - ment to a - rise. __

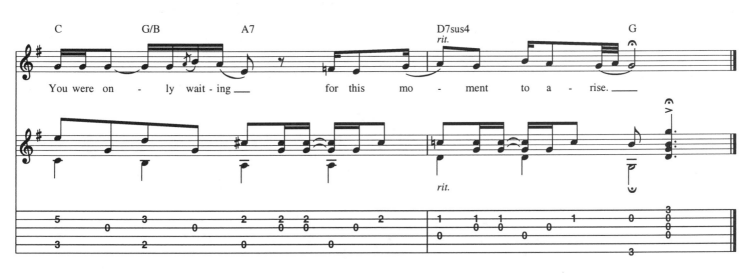

You were on - ly wait-ing __ for this mo - ment to a - rise. __

Blue on Black

Words and Music by Kenny Wayne Shepherd, Tia Sillers and Mark Selby

MCA Music Publishing

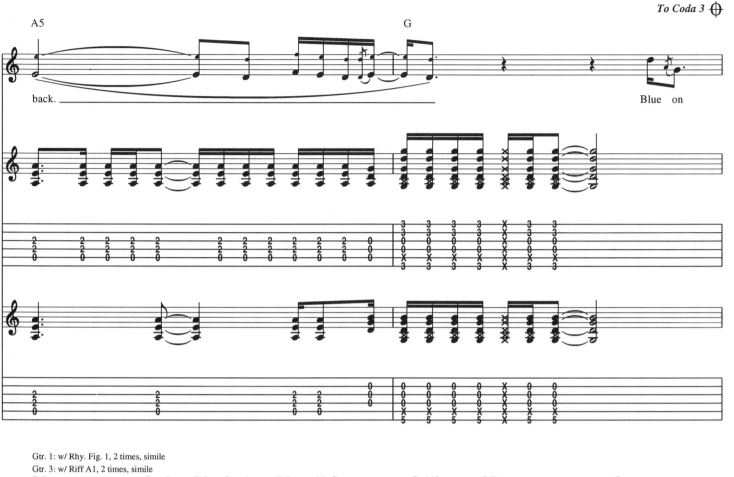

back. _____

Blue on

Gtr. 1: w/ Rhy. Fig. 1, 2 times, simile
Gtr. 3: w/ Riff A1, 2 times, simile

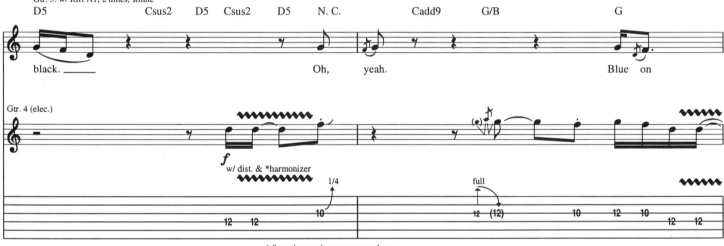

black. _____

Oh, yeah.

Blue on

Gtr. 4 (elec.)

f w/ dist. & *harmonizer

* Set to harmonize one octave above.

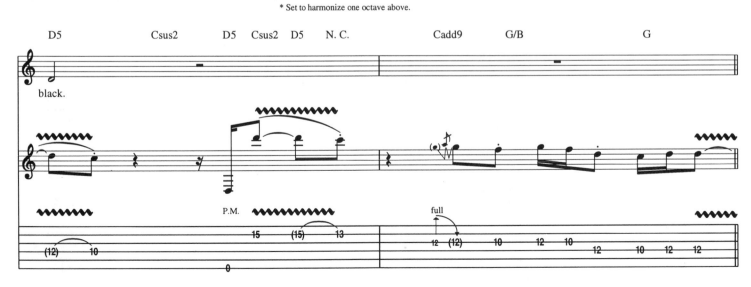

black.

10

Verse

Gtr. 1: w/ Rhy. Fig. 1, 8 times, simile
Gtr. 3: w/ Riff A1, 8 times, simile

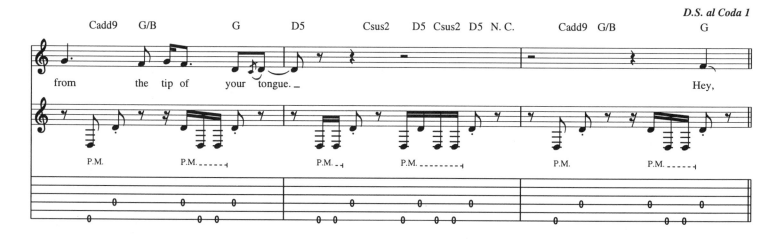

⊕ *Coda 1*

Gtr. 1: w/ Rhy. Fig. 1, 2 times, simile
Gtr. 3: w/ Riff A1, 2 times, simile

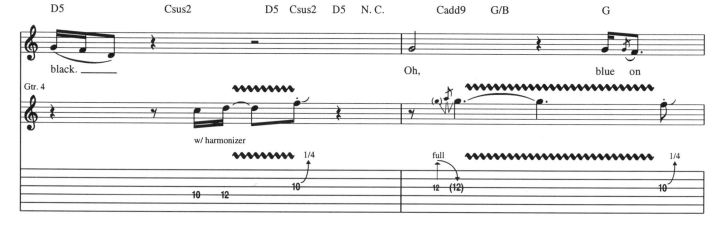

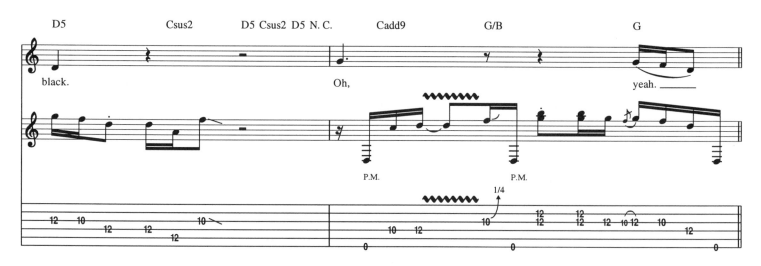

Guitar Solo

Gtr. 1: w/ Rhy. Fig.1, 6 times, simile
Gtr. 3: w/ Riff A1, 6 times, simile

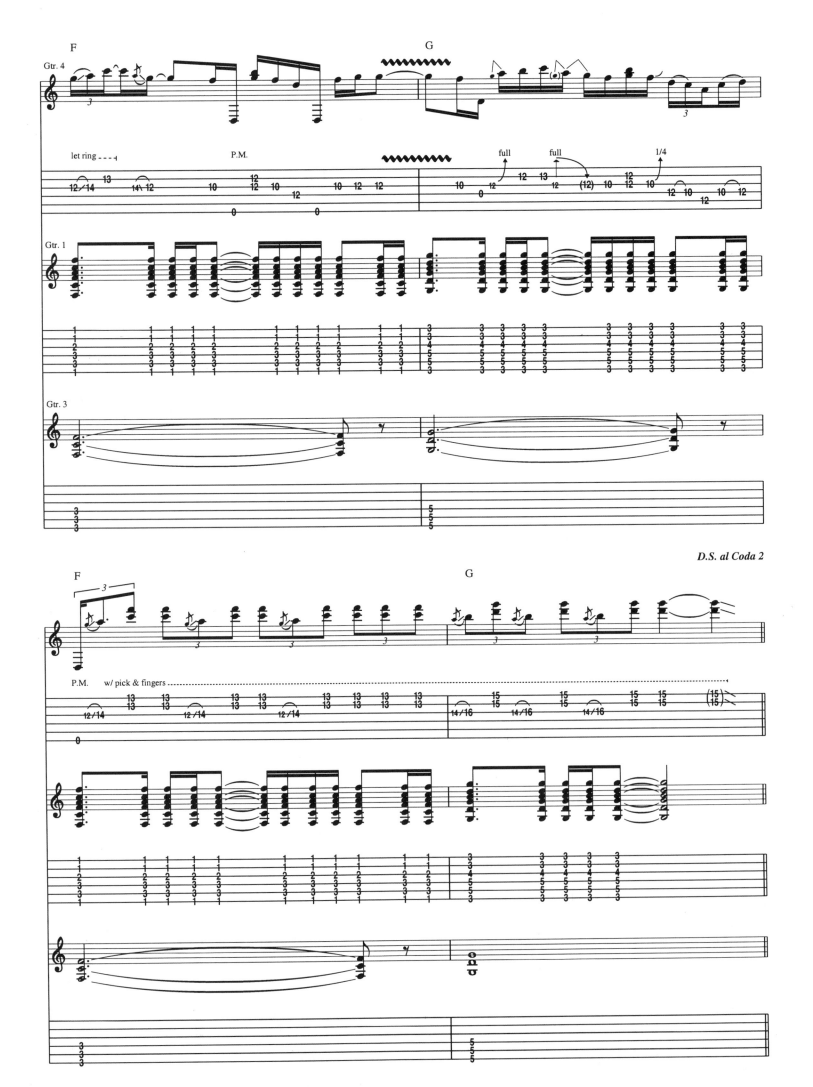

D.S. al Coda 2

Give Me One Reason

Words and Music by Tracy Chapman

Guitar Solo

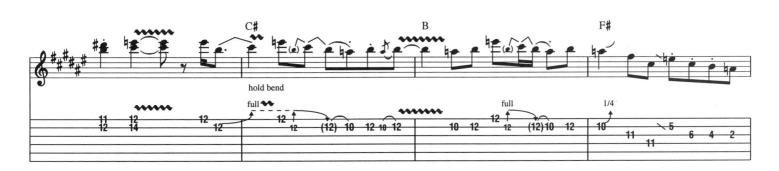

Verse

5. This youth-ful heart can love you, __ yes, and give you what you need. _____

I said this youth-ful heart can love you, __ ho, and give you what you need. _____

But I'm too old to go chas-in' you a - round, wast-in' my pre-cious en-er-gy.

Verse

Gtr. 1: w/ Rhy. Fig. 1

6. Give me one rea-son to stay here, __ yes, now turn right back a-round. (A -

round. __ You can see the turn in me.) Give me one rea-son to stay here __

oh, I'll turn right back a - round. _

(You can see the turn in me.) Said I

Gtr. 2 tacet

don't wan - na leave you lone - ly, _____ you _____ got to make me change my

Hey Joe

Words and Music by Billy Roberts

you know I caught her mess-in' 'round with an-oth-er   man.

Yeah!

Ooh.

I'm go-in' down to shoot my old la-dy,

wom-an down, you shot her down, now.

Uh, hey, ___ Joe,

Ah. ___

I heard you shot your old

la - dy down, _ you shot her down in the ground. _   Yeah! _

Yes, I __ did,   I shot her,   you know I caught her mess - in' 'round,

Ah. _____

mess - in' 'round   town. __

C   Gadd9   D   A

Uh, yes I did, I   shot her,   you know I   caught my old la - dy mess-in' 'round
Ah. __

Shoot her one more time a - gain, _ ba - by!

Ooh. _____

Hey, Joe! _____)

Yeah!

Ah, dig it!

Sweet Child O' Mine

Words and Music by W. Axl Rose, Slash, Izzy Stradlin', Duff McKagan and Steven Adler

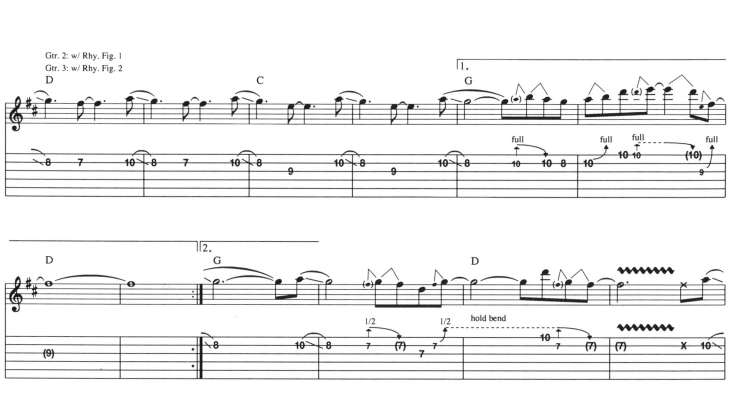

Oh, oh,— oh, oh,——— sweet child_ o' mine.———

Woo,— yeah,— yeah! Ooh,——————— sweet love o' mine.————

Guitar Solo

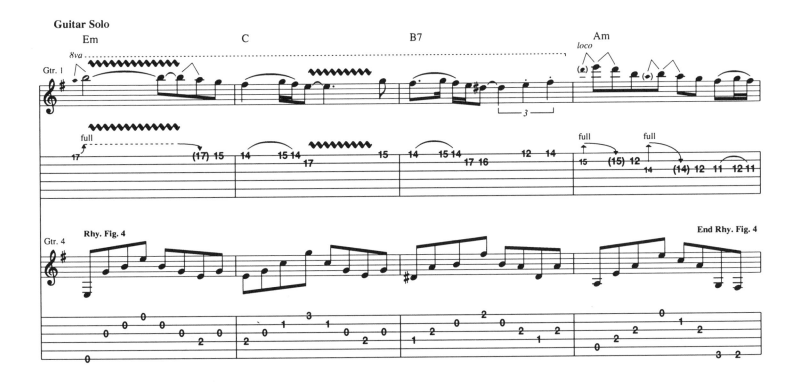

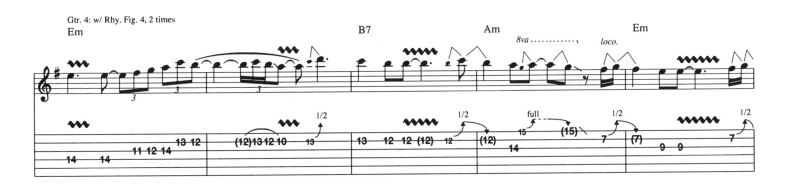

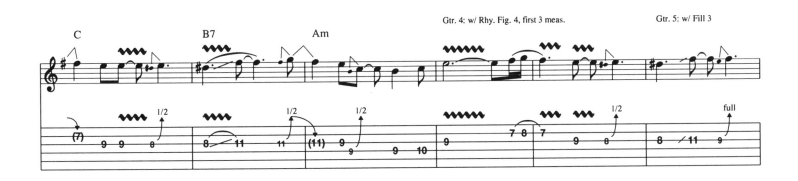

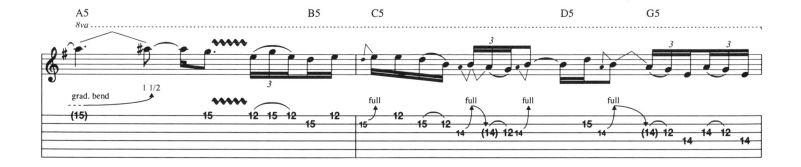

Gtr. 2: w/ Rhy. Fig. 6, 2 times

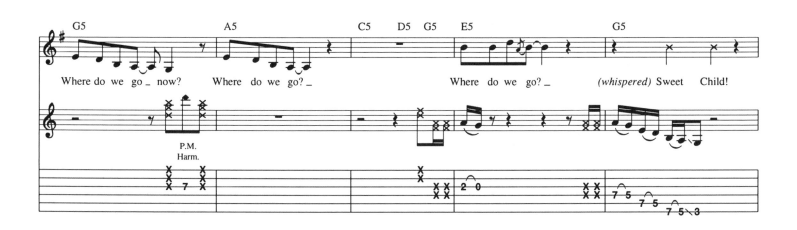

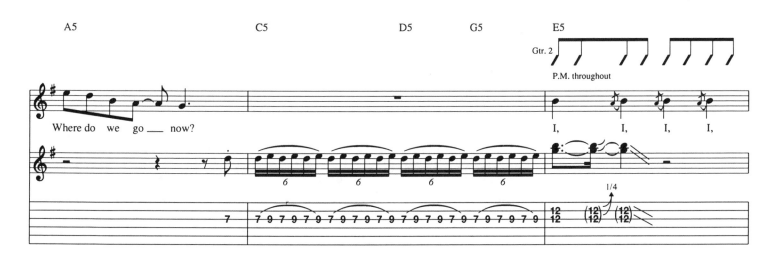

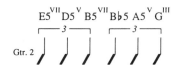

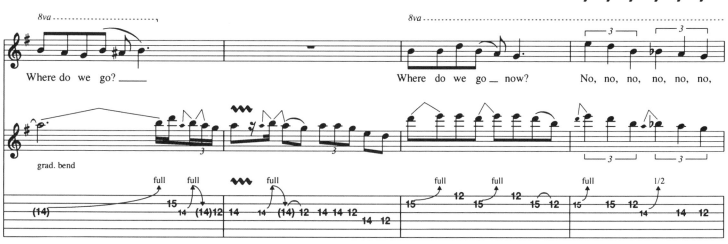

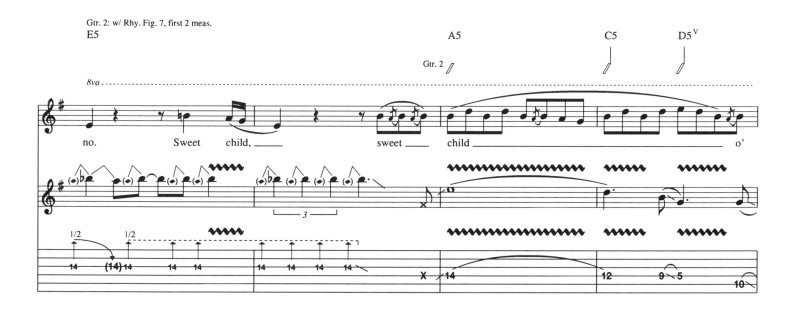

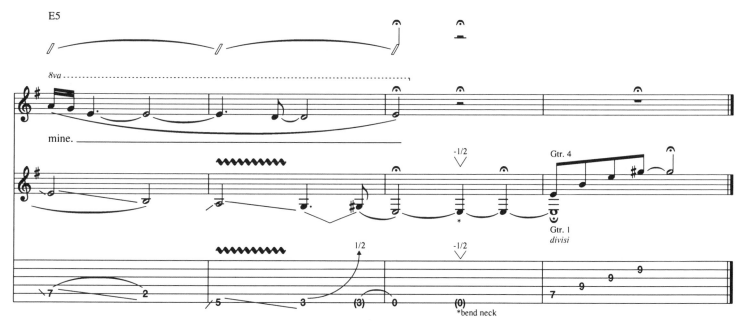

Sweet Home Alabama

Words and Music by Ronnie Van Zant, Ed King and Gary Rossington

MCA Music Publishing

Well, I hope Neil Young will re-mem - ber,   a south- ern man _ don't need him a -

—   Ooh,   ooh,   ooh.   South ern   man don't need him a -

ooh.

Chorus

round,   an-y-how.   Sweet _ home Al - a-bam-a,

round.)

where the skies   are so blue. _   Sweet _ home Al - a-

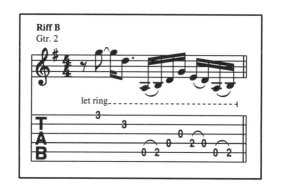

bam - a,   Lord, I'm com-in'   home   to   you.

Guitar Solo

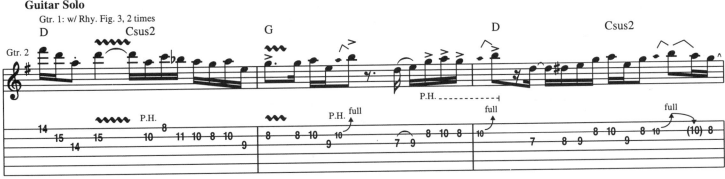

Verse

3. In Bir-ming-ham _ they love the gov - 'nor,   boo,   boo,

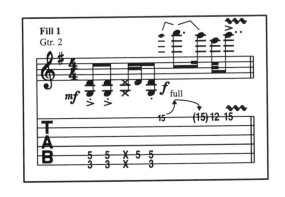

Gtr. 2: w/ Riff A, last 2 meas. only

hoo. Now we all did __ what we could do.

Now Wa-ter-gate __ does not

both __ er me,

does your con-science both-er you? __ Tell the truth.

Chorus

Gtr. 1: w/ Rhy. Fig. 2, 1st 6 meas.
Gtr. 2: w/ Rhy. Fig. 2A

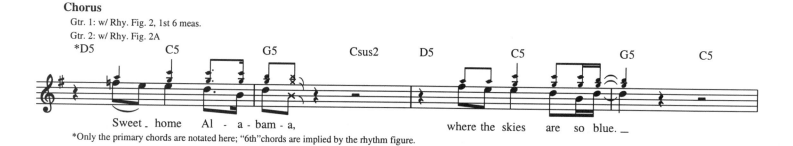

*D5   C5   G5   Csus2   D5   C5   G5   C5

Sweet __ home Al - a - bam - a,

where the skies are so blue. __

*Only the primary chords are notated here; "6th" chords are implied by the rhythm figure.

D5   C5   G5   Csus2 D5   C5   G5

Gtr. 1: w/ Rhy. Fig. 4

Gtr. 2: w/ Fill 2 (see p. ?)

Sweet __ home Al - a - bam - a,   yeah.

Lord, I'm com-in' home to you. Here I come.   Al - a - bam - a!

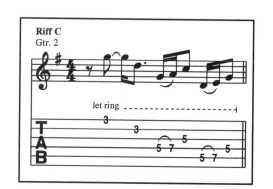

Riff C
Gtr. 2

let ring

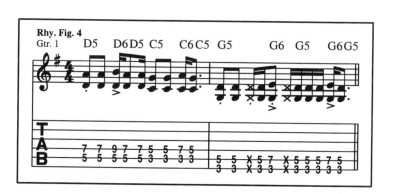

Rhy. Fig. 4
Gtr. 1   D5   D6 D5 C5   C6 C5 G5   G6   G5   G6 G5

Guitar Solo

Gtr. 1: w/ Rhy. Fig. 4

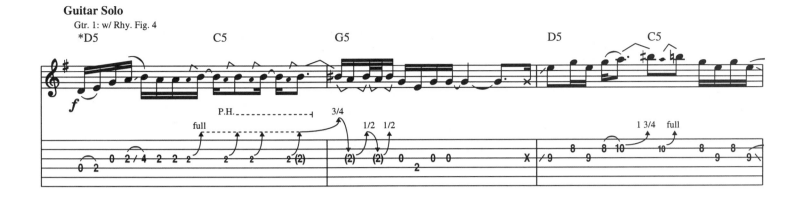

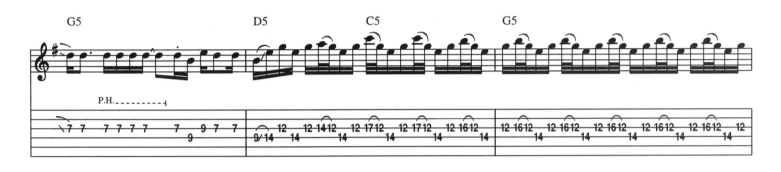

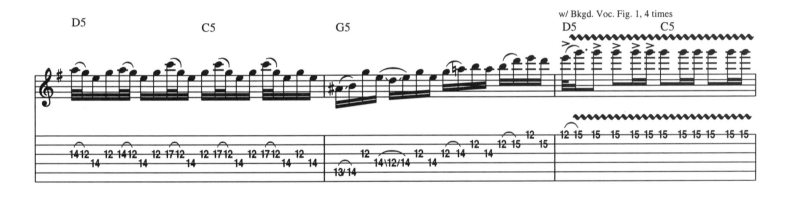

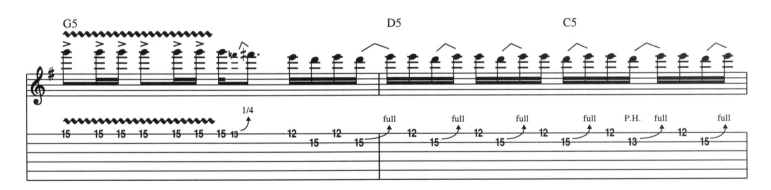

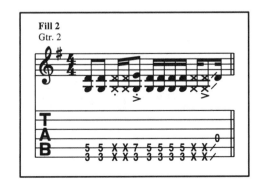

Ah, ah, ah, Al-a-bam-a!

53

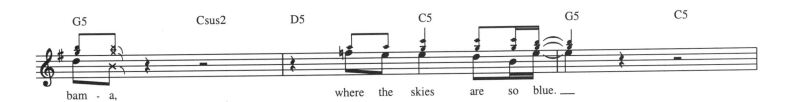

bam - a,   where the skies   are   so   blue. ___

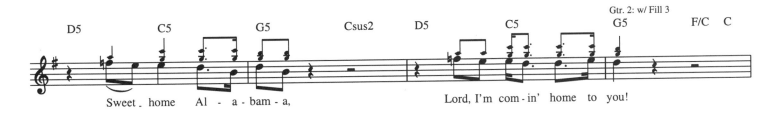

Sweet __ home Al - a - bam - a,   Lord, I'm com - in' home to you!

Gtr. 1: w/ Rhy. Fig. 2
Gtr. 2: w/ Rhy. Fig. 2A

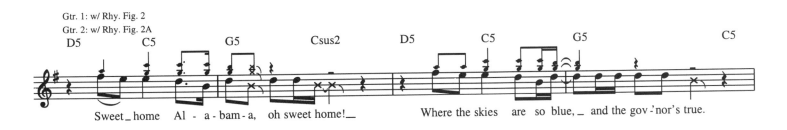

Sweet __ home Al - a - bam - a, oh sweet home! ___   Where the skies   are   so   blue, __ and the gov -'nor's true.

Gtrs. 1 & 2: w/ Rhy. Fig. 4

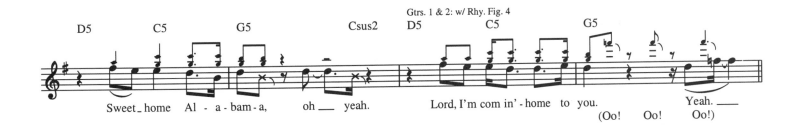

Sweet __ home Al - a - bam - a,   oh ___ yeah.   Lord, I'm com in' - home to you.   Yeah. ___
                                                                      (Oo!   Oo!   Oo!)

Play 6 times and Fade

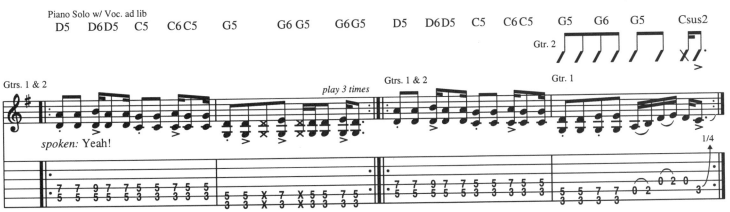

spoken: Yeah!

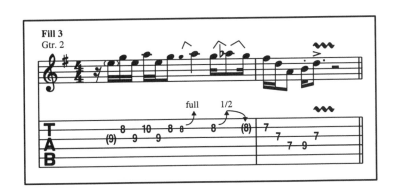

from *Deepest Purple - The Very Best of Deep Purple*

Smoke on the Water

**Words and Music by Ritchie Blackmore, Ian Gillan,
Roger Glover, Jon Lord and Ian Paice**

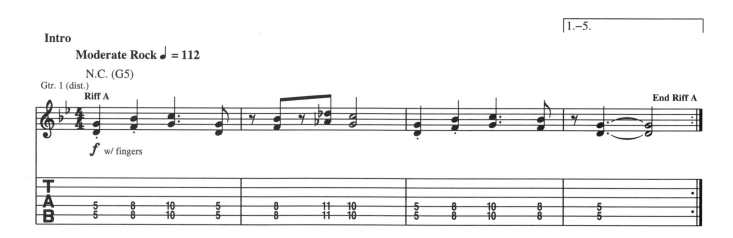

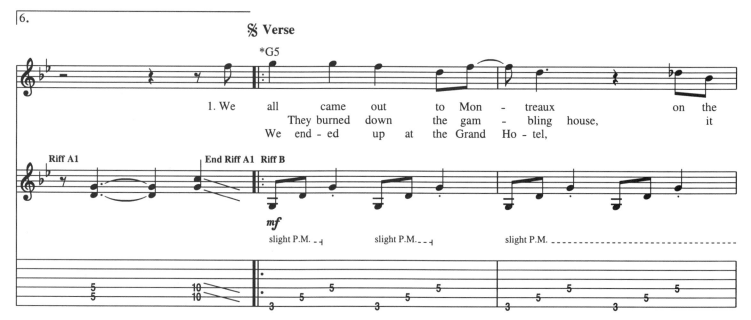

*Chord symbols reflect implied tonality.

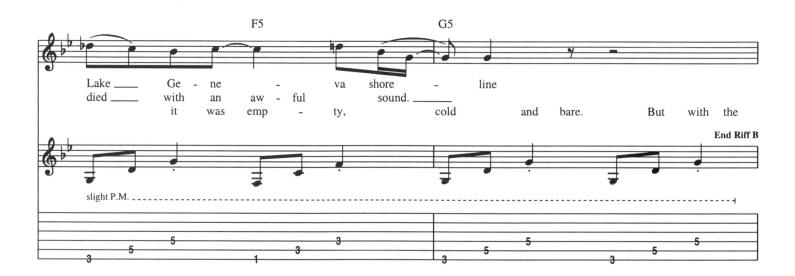

Gtr. 1: w/ Riff B, 3 times, simile

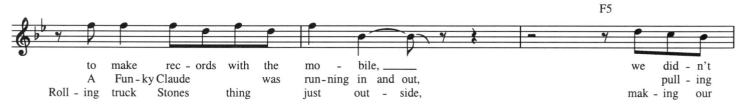

F5

to make rec - ords with the mo - bile, _____ we did - n't
A Fun - ky Claude was run - ning in and out, pull - ing
Roll - ing truck Stones thing just out - side, mak - ing our

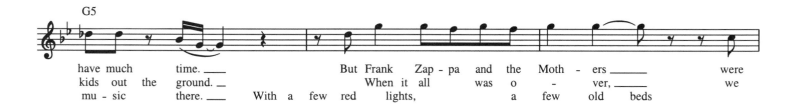

G5

have much time. ____ But Frank Zap - pa and the Moth - ers _____ were
kids out the ground. _ When it all was o - ver, _____ we
mu - sic there. ____ With a few red lights, a few old beds

F5   G5

at the best place a - round. _____ But some stu - pid with a
had to find an - oth - er place. _____ But Swiss time was
we made a place to sweat. _____ No mat - ter what we

F5   G5

flare gun burned the place to the _____ ground. ____
run - ning out; it seemed that we would lose the race. ____
get out of this, I know, I know we'll nev - er for - get.

Chorus

C   Ab5   G5

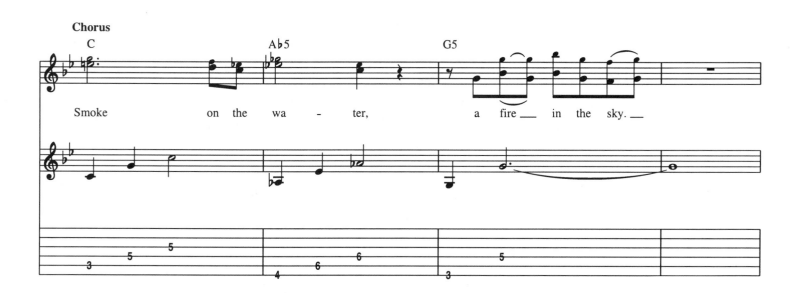

Smoke on the wa - ter, a fire ___ in the sky. ___

57

60

⊕ *Coda*

Outro-Organ Solo

Gtr. 1: w/ Riff A, 4 times

N.C.(G5)　　　　　　　　N.C.(G5)

Begin Fade

Fade Out

Wild Thing

Words and Music by Chip Taylor

Recorder Solo

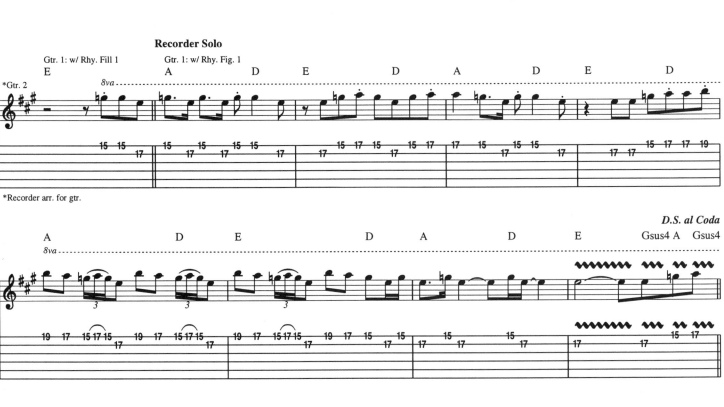

*Recorder arr. for gtr.

D.S. al Coda

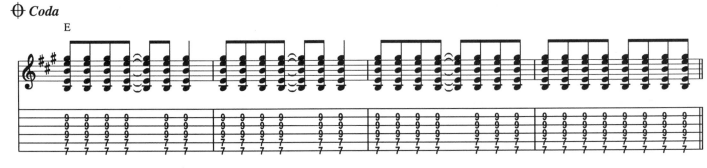

⊕ *Coda*

Outro-Chorus

Gtr. 1: w/ Rhy. Fig. 1, 1st 2 meas., till fade

Wild thing,   you make my heart sing.   You make ev - 'ry-thing groov - y. __

__   Wild thing.   Come on, _ come on wild thing.

Begin Fade   *Fade Out*

Shake it, _ shake it, wild thing.   I love _ you, wild thing.

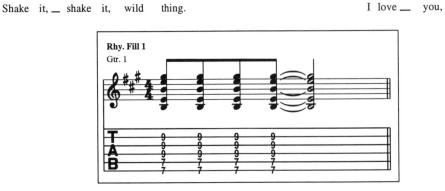

Rhy. Fill 1
Gtr. 1

Building a Mystery

Words and Music by Sarah McLachlan and Pierre Marchand

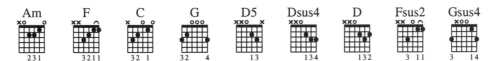

Am   F   C   G   D5   Dsus4   D   Fsus2   Gsus4

* Strum Pattern: 1, 3
* Pick Pattern: 3, 4

Intro
Moderately Slow

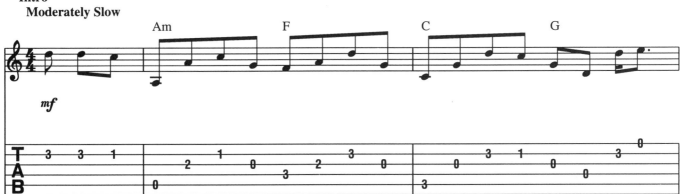

mf

* use pattern 10 for ⅜ meas.

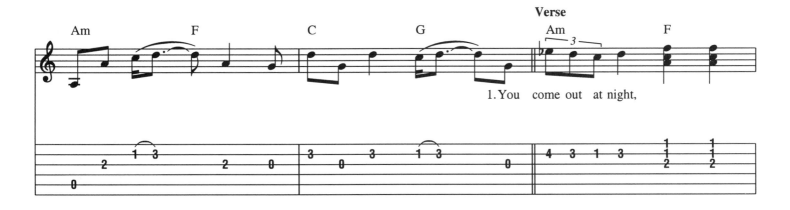

Verse

1.You come out at night,

that's when the en- er- gy comes _ and the dark side's light, and the

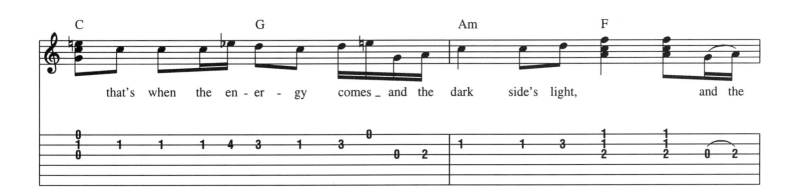

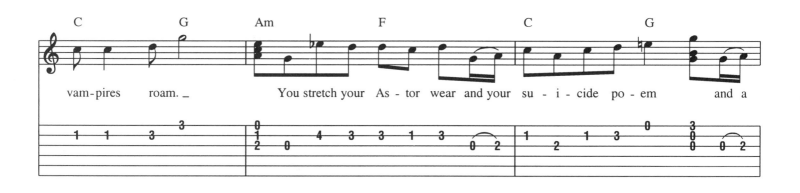

vam-pires roam. _ You stretch your As - tor wear and your su - i - cide po - em and a

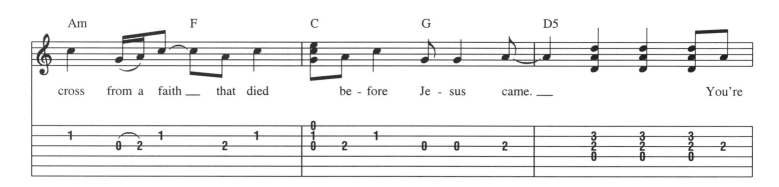

cross from a faith __ that died be - fore Je - sus came. __ You're

Interlude

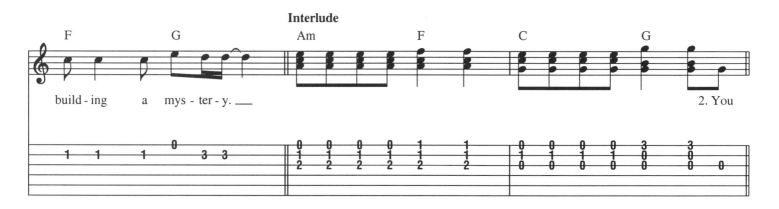

build - ing a mys - ter - y. __ 2. You

Verse

live in a church where you sleep with voo - doo dolls, ___ and you
3. See Additional Lyrics

won't give up the search ___ for the ghost in the halls. ___

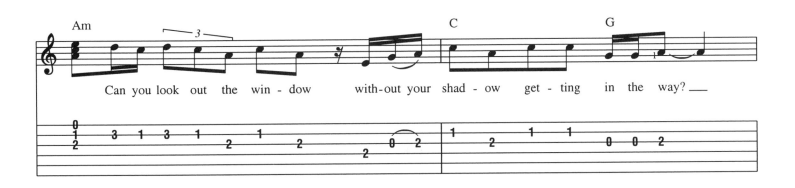

Chorus

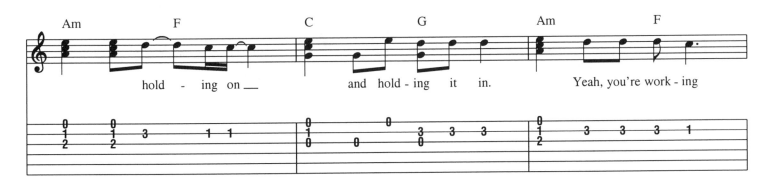

Additional Lyrics

3. You woke up screaming aloud
   A prayer from your secret god to
   Feed off of fears and hold back your tears, oh.
   You give us a tantrum and a know-it-all grin
   Just when you need one, when the evenin' stayed.
   You're a beautiful, a beautiful fucked up man.
   You set it up, you're razor wire sharp.

All the Things You Are

Lyrics by Oscar Hammerstein II
Music by Jerome Kern

Candle in the Wind

Music by Elton John
Words by Bernie Taupin

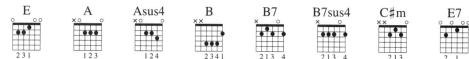

Strum Pattern: 3
Pick Pattern: 2

Verse
Slowly

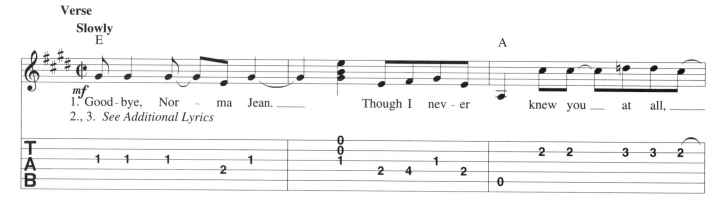

1. Good-bye, Nor - ma Jean. _____ Though I nev - er knew you _ at all,
2., 3. *See Additional Lyrics*

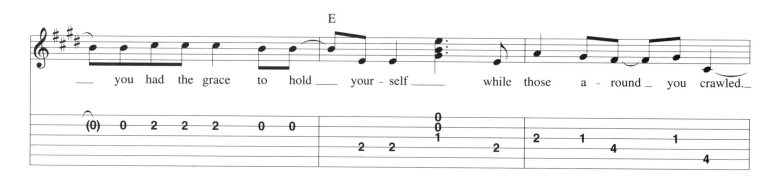

_____ you had the grace to hold _____ your - self _____ while those a - round _ you crawled. _

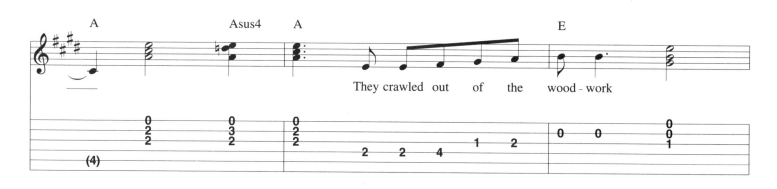

They crawled out of the wood - work

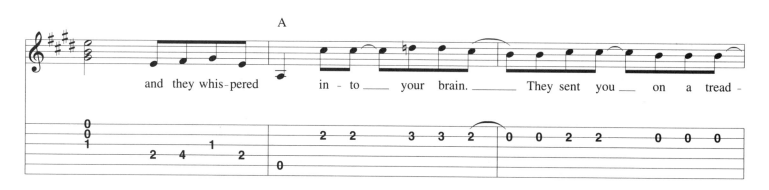

and they whis-pered in - to _____ your brain. _____ They sent you _ on a tread -

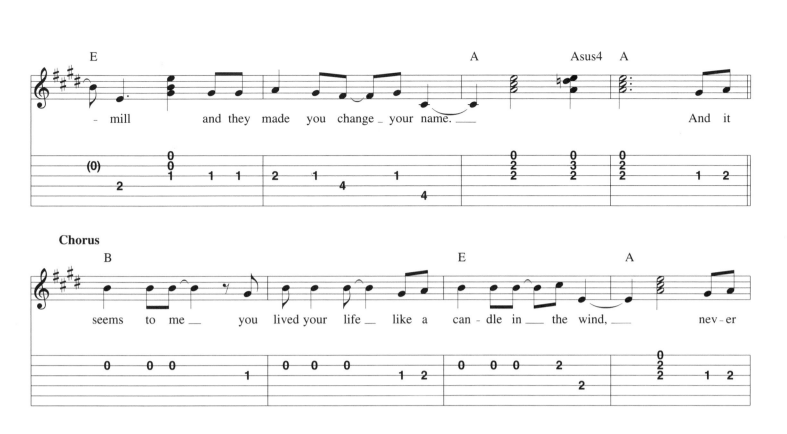

Chorus

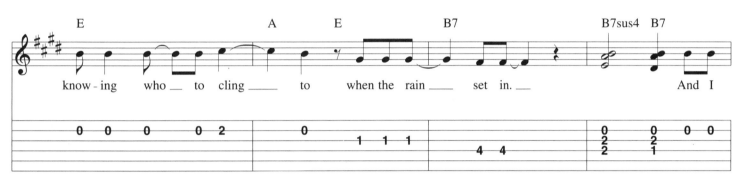

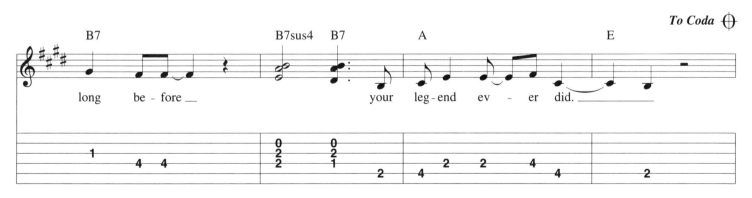

Additional Lyrics

2. Loneliness was tough, the toughest role you ever played.
   Hollywood created a superstar and pain was the price you paid.
   And even when you died, oh, the press still hounded you.
   All the papers had to say was that Marilyn was found in the nude.

3. Goodbye, Norma Jean. Though I never knew you at all,
   You had the grace to hold yourself while those around you crawled.
   Goodbye, Norma Jean, from a young man in the twenty second row,
   Who sees you as something more than sexual, more than just our Marilyn Monroe.

Can't Smile Without You

Words and Music by Chris Arnold, David Martin and Geoff Morrow

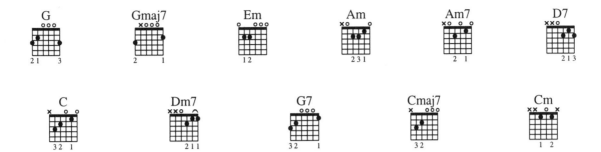

Strum Pattern: 3
Pick Pattern: 2

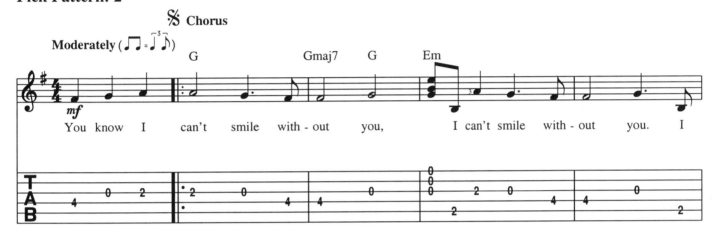

You know I can't smile with-out you, I can't smile with-out you. I

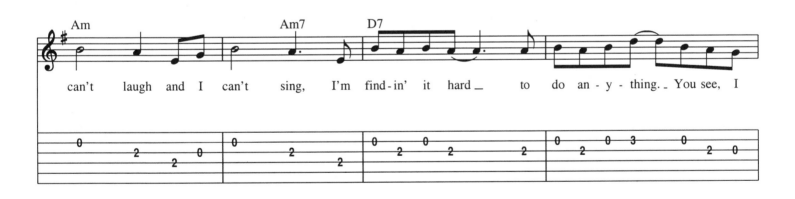

can't laugh and I can't sing, I'm find-in' it hard __ to do an-y-thing. You see, I

feel sad when you're sad, I feel glad when you're glad. If

To Coda 1
To Coda 2

you on-ly knew what I'm go-in' through, I just can't smile _____ with-out

Verse

you. _____ 1. You came a - long _____ just like a song _ and

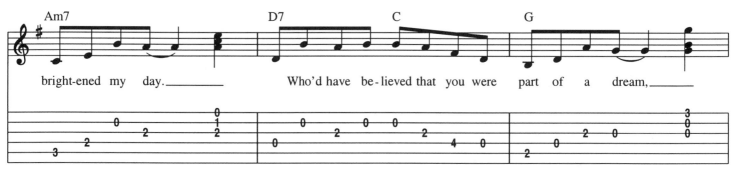

bright-ened my day._____ Who'd have be - lieved that you were part of a dream,_____

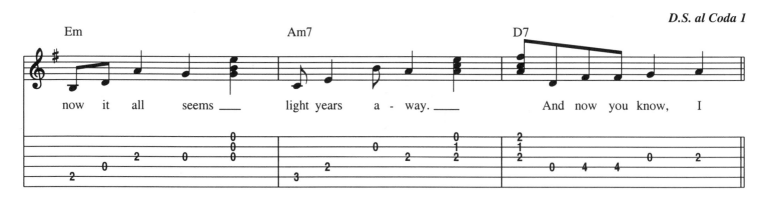

D.S. al Coda 1

now it all seems ___ light years a - way. ___ And now you know, I

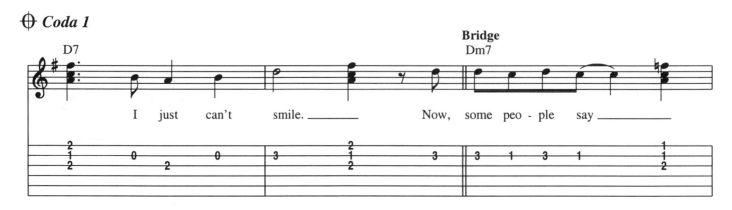

Coda 1

Bridge

I just can't smile. _____ Now, some peo - ple say _____

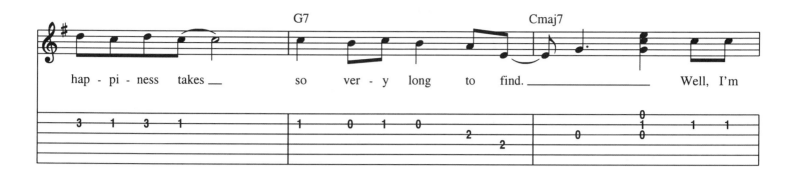

hap - pi - ness takes ___ so ver - y long to find. _____ Well, I'm

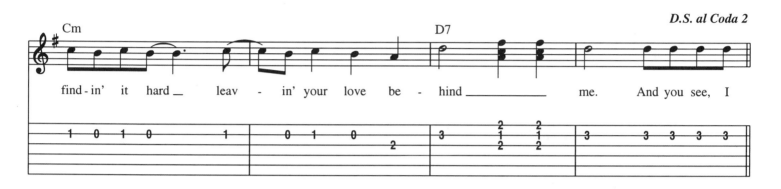

D.S. al Coda 2

find - in' it hard ___ leav - in' your love be - hind _____ me. And you see, I

⊕ *Coda 2*

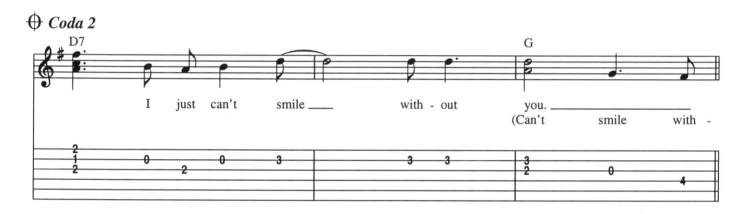

I just can't smile ___ with - out you. _____
(Can't smile with -

Outro

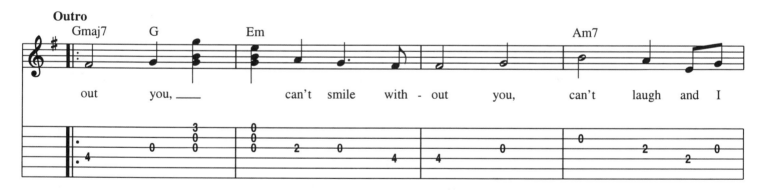

out you, ___ can't smile with - out you, can't laugh and I

Repeat and Fade

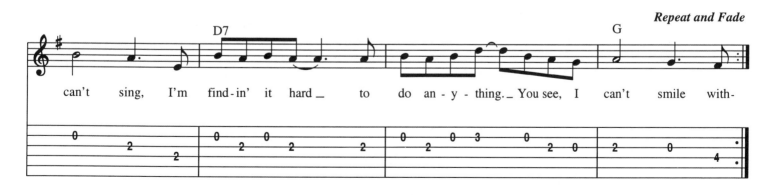

can't sing, I'm find - in' it hard ___ to do an - y - thing. ___ You see, I can't smile with -

Circle of Life

from Walt Disney Pictures' THE LION KING

Music by Elton John
Lyrics by Tim Rice

Strum Pattern: 2
Pick Pattern: 2

Day Tripper

Words and Music by John Lennon and Paul McCartney

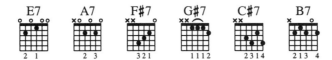

Strum Pattern: 2, 5
Pick Pattern: 4

Intro

Moderate Rock

Verse

1. Got a good rea - son
2., 3. *See Additional Lyrics*

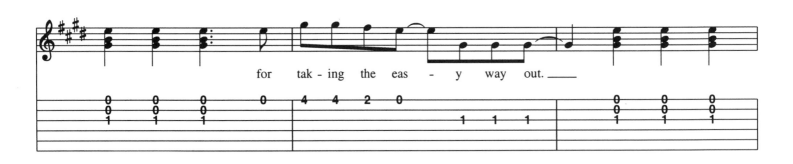

for tak - ing the eas - y way out. _____

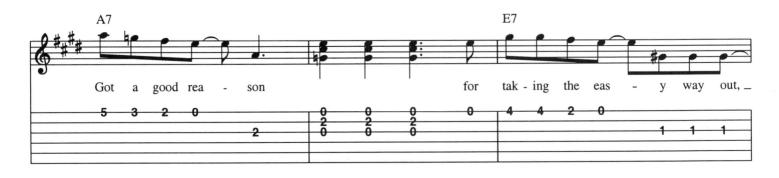

Got a good rea - son   for tak - ing the eas - y way out, _

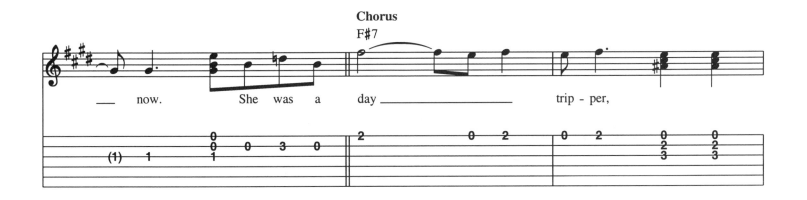

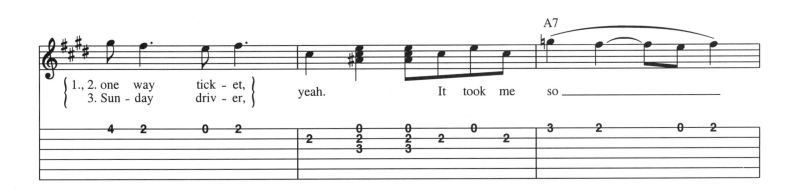

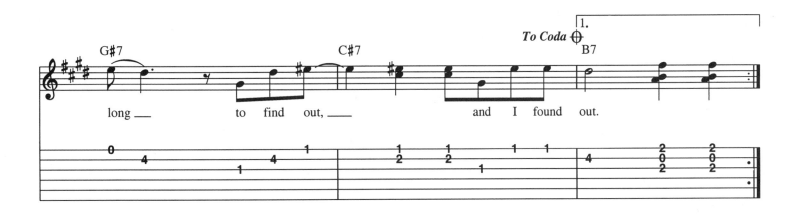

Guitar Solo

D.C. al Coda

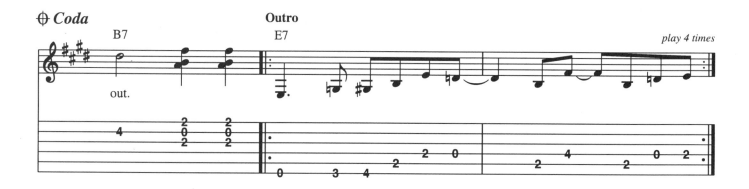

Outro

play 4 times

Repeat and Fade

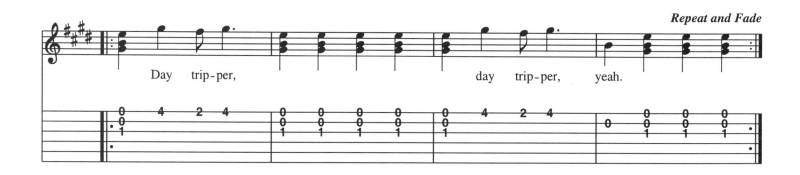

Day trip-per, day trip-per, yeah.

Additional Lyrics

2. She's a big teaser.
   She took me half the way there.
   She's a big teaser.
   She took me half the way there, now.

3. Tried to please her.
   She only played one night stands.
   Tried to please her.
   She only played one night stands, now.

Ebony and Ivory

Words and Music by McCartney

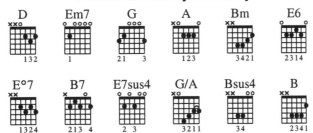

Strum Pattern: 1, 4
Pick Pattern: 1, 2

Chorus
Moderately

mp

Eb - on - y ___ and i - vo - ry ___ live to - geth - er in per - fect

har - mo - ny, ___ side by side on my pian - o key-board, oh ___ Lord,

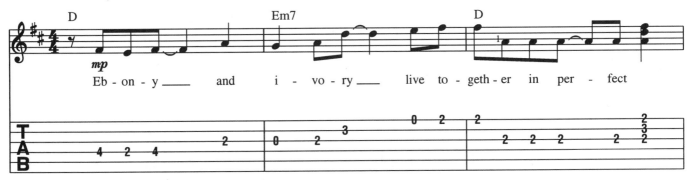

To Coda 1 ⊕

why don't we? ___

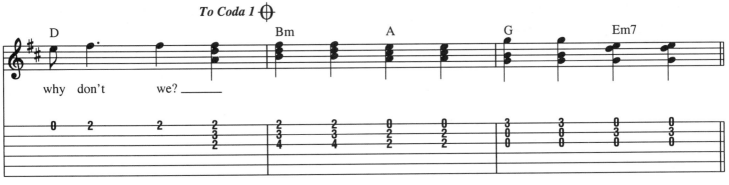

Verse

1., 2. We all know _ that peo - ple are the same wher - ev - er you go. ___ There is

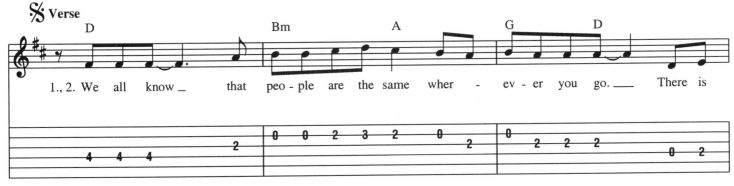

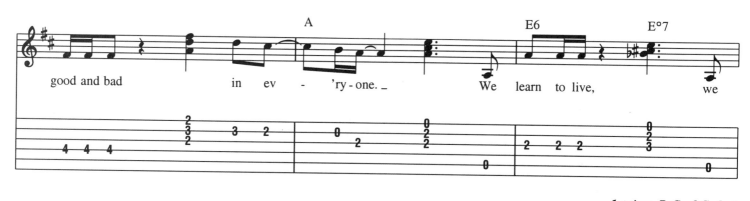

good and bad   in ev - 'ry-one. __   We   learn   to live,   we

1st time, D.C. al Coda 1
2nd time, To Coda 2 ⊕

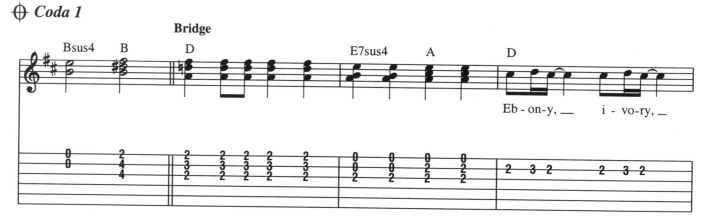

learn   to give each oth - er what we need __ to sur - vive __   to - geth - er   a - live. _____

⊕ *Coda 1*

Bridge

Eb - on - y, __   i - vo - ry, __

D.S. al Coda 2

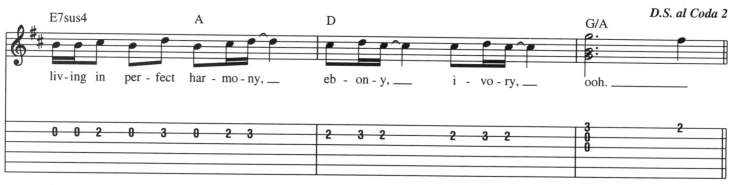

liv - ing in per - fect har - mo - ny, __   eb - on - y, __   i - vo - ry, __   ooh. _____

⊕ *Coda 2*

Chorus

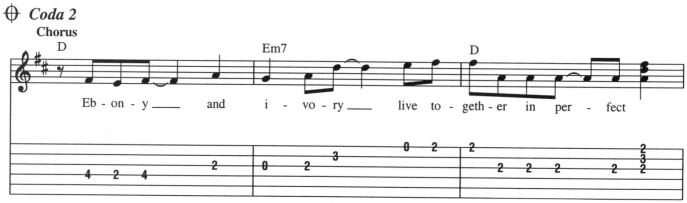

Eb - on - y _____ and   i - vo - ry _____ live to - geth - er in per - fect

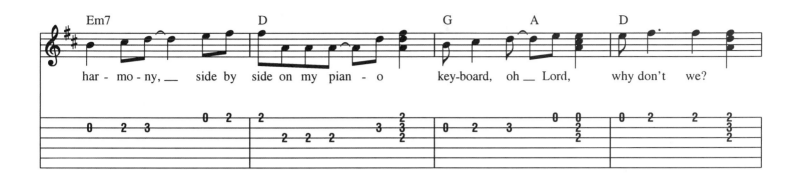

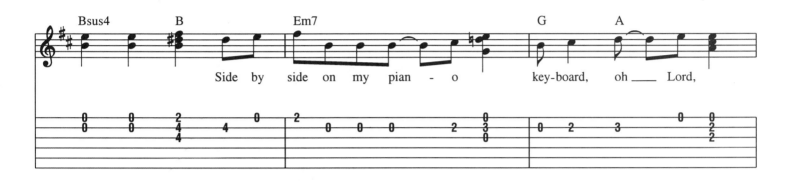

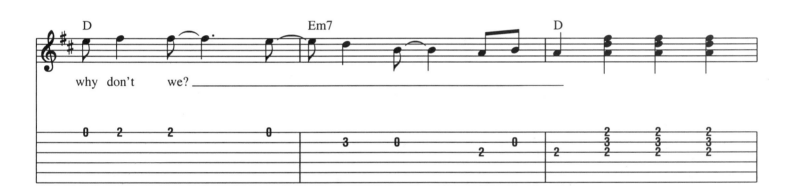

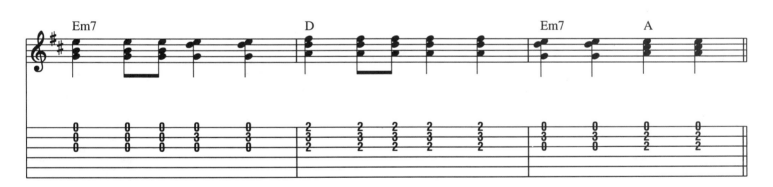

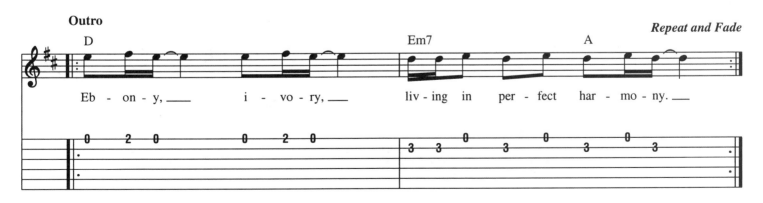

85

Endless Love

from ENDLESS LOVE

Words and Music by Lionel Richie

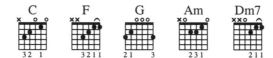

Strum Pattern: 3
Pick Pattern: 3

Verse
Rock Ballad

1. My love, there's on-ly you in my life, _____
2. *See Additional Lyrics*

the on-ly thing that's right. My first love,

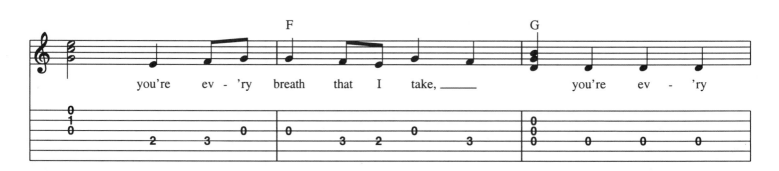

you're ev-'ry breath that I take, _____ you're ev-'ry

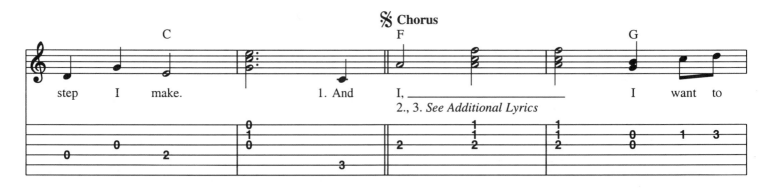

step I make. 1. And I, _____ I want to
2., 3. *See Additional Lyrics*

𝄋 Chorus

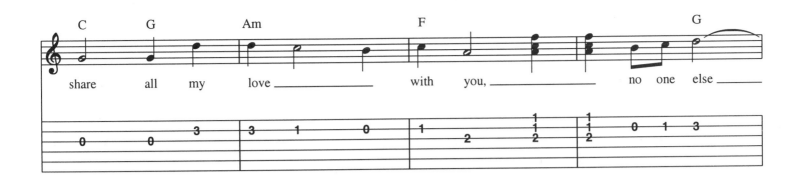

share all my love _____ with you, _____ no one else _____

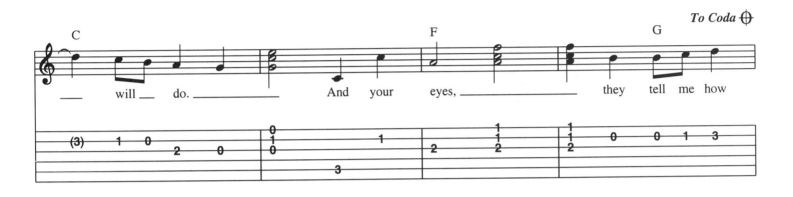

_____ will _____ do. _____ And your eyes, _____ they tell me how

To Coda ⊕

1.

much you care. _____ Oh, _____ yes, _____ you will al - ways be, _____

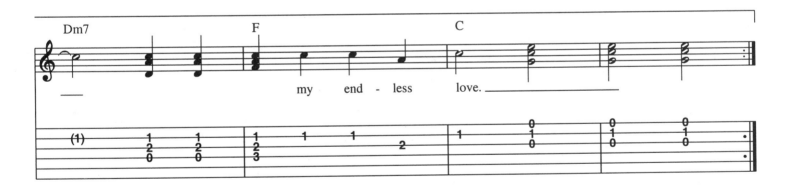

_____ my end - less love. _____

2.

world to me. _____ Oh, I know _____ I found in

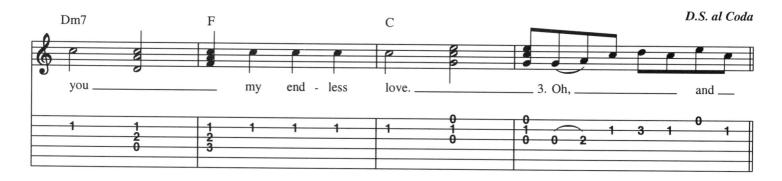

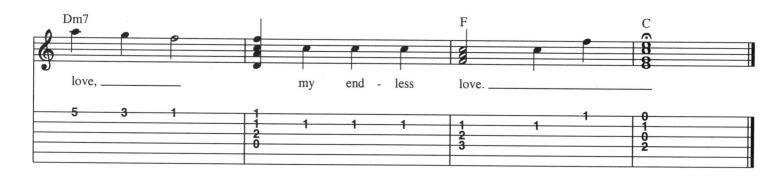

Additional Lyrics

2. Two hearts, two hearts that beat as one,
Our lives have just begun.
Forever I hold you close in my arms,
I can't resist your charms.

Chorus 2. And love, I'd be a fool for you,
I'm sure you know I don't mind.
'Cause you, you mean the world to me.
Oh, I know I found in you,
My endless love.

Chorus 3. Oh, and love, I'd be a fool for you,
I'm sure you know I don't mind.
And yes, you'll be the only one.

Forever in Love

By Kenny G

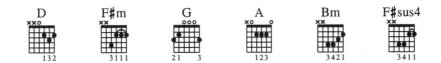

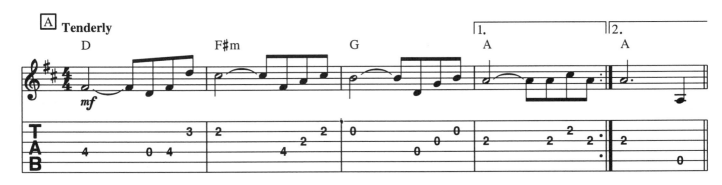

Strum Pattern: 4
Pick Pattern: 2

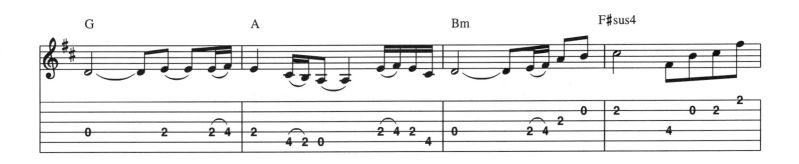

Every Breath You Take

Written and Composed by Sting

Strum Pattern: 4
Pick Pattern: 3

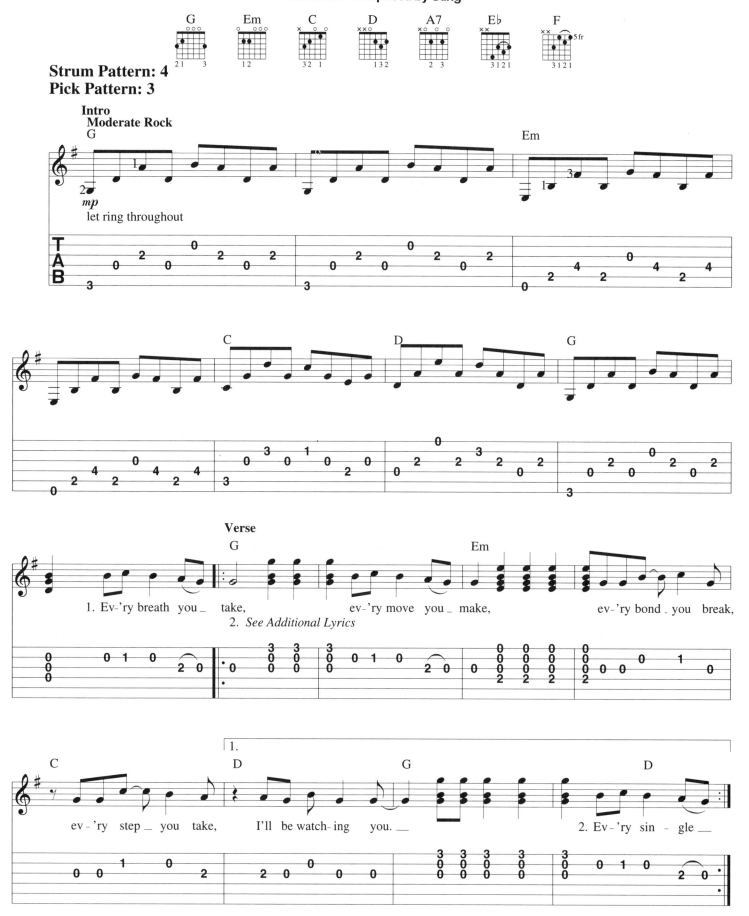

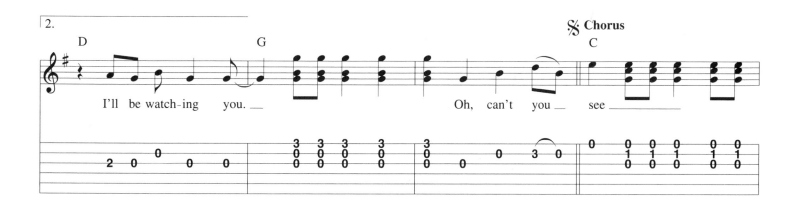

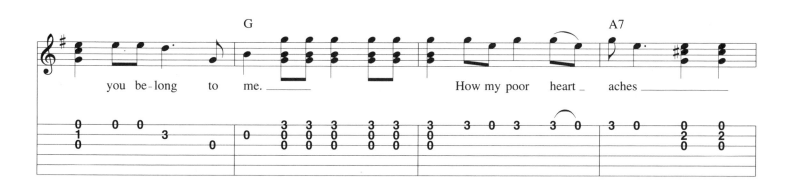

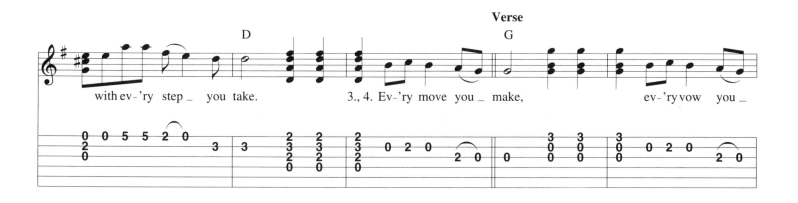

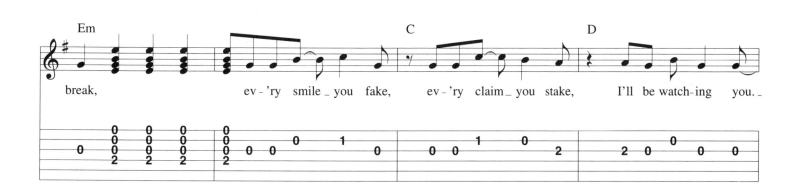

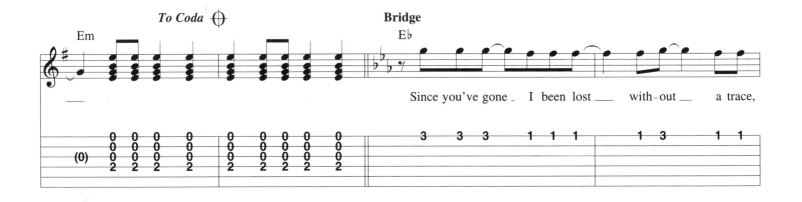

Since you've gone _ I been lost _ with-out _ a trace,

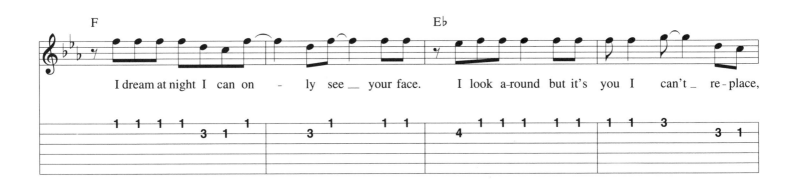

I dream at night I can on - ly see _ your face. I look a-round but it's you I can't _ re-place,

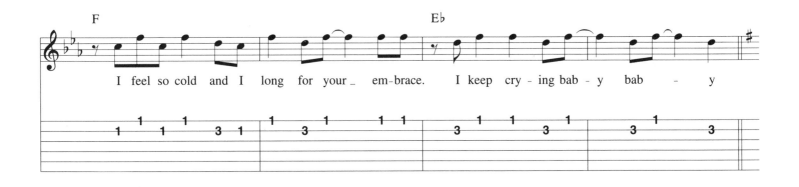

I feel so cold and I long for your _ em-brace. I keep cry - ing bab - y bab - y

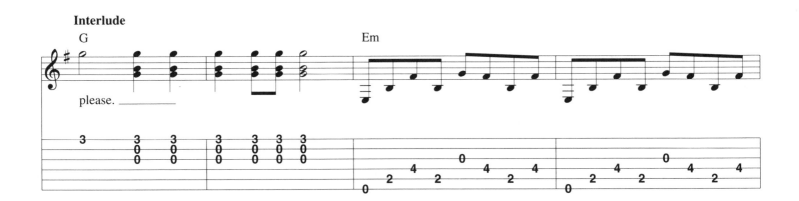

please. _____

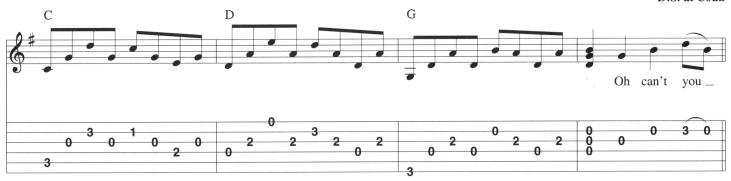

Oh can't you _

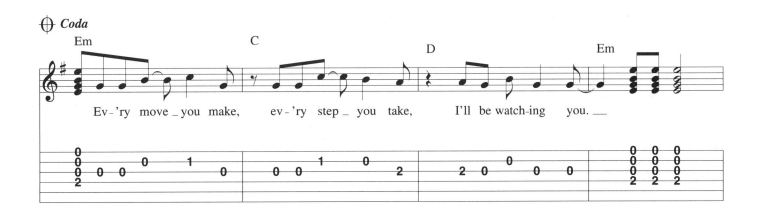

$\oplus$ *Coda*

Ev-'ry move _ you make, ev-'ry step _ you take, I'll be watch-ing you. _

I'll be watch-ing you. _____

Additional Lyrics

2. Ev'ry single day, ev'ry word you say,
   Ev'ry game you play, ev'ry night you stay,
   I'll be watching you.

Für Elise

Music by Ludwig Van Beethoven

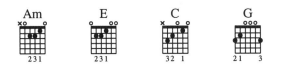

Strum Pattern: 7, 9
Pick Pattern: 7, 9

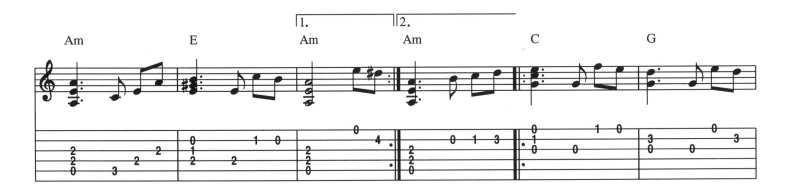

I've Got Peace Like a River

Traditional

Strum Pattern: 3
Pick Pattern: 3

Joyously

Verse

1. I've got peace like a riv-er, I've got peace like a
2., 3. *See Additional Lyrics*

riv-er, I've got peace like a riv-er in my soul. _____ I've got

peace like a riv-er, I've got peace like a riv-er, I've got

peace like a riv-er in __ my soul. (My soul.) 2. I've got soul. (My soul.)

Additional Lyrics

2. I've got love like an ocean,
   I've got love like an ocean,
   I've got love like an ocean in my soul.
   I've got love like an ocean,
   I've got love like an ocean,
   I've got love like an ocean in my soul. (My soul.)

3. I've got joy like a fountain,
   I've got joy like a fountain,
   I've got joy like a fountain in my soul.
   I've got joy like a fountain,
   I've got joy like a fountain,
   I've got joy like a fountain in my soul. (My soul.)

Imagine

Words and Music by John Lennon

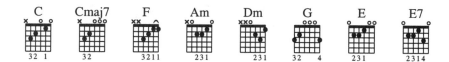

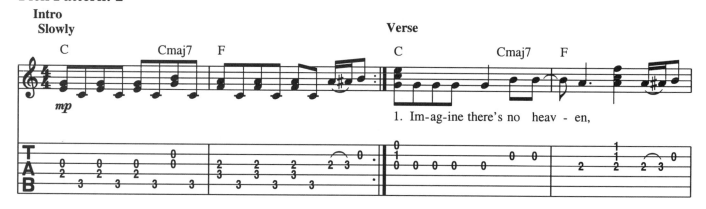

Strum Pattern: 1
Pick Pattern: 2

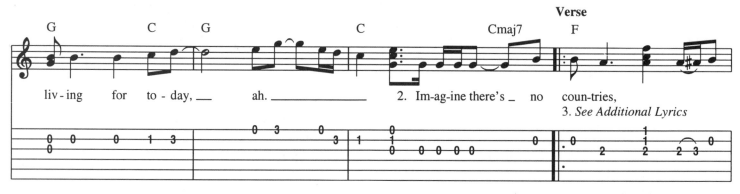

Additional Lyrics

3. Imagine no possessions,
   I wonder if you can;
   No need for greed or hunger,
   A brotherhood of man.
   Imagine all the people sharing all the world.

Jailhouse Rock

Words and Music by Jerry Leiber and Mike Stoller

Strum Pattern: 3
Pick Pattern: 3

Chorus

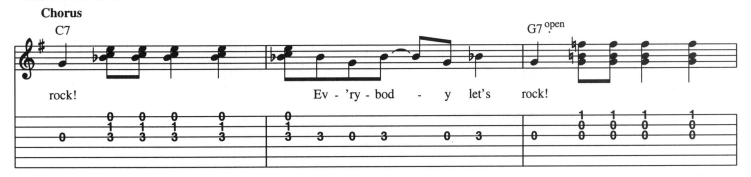

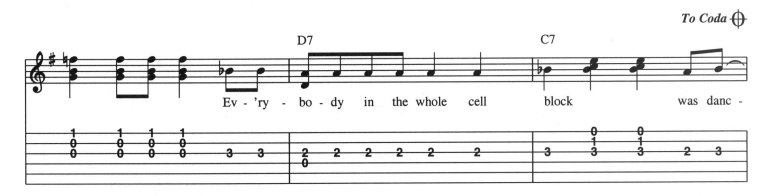

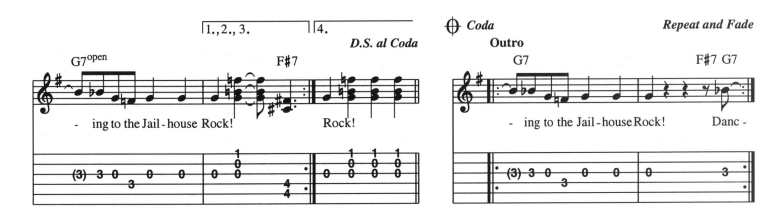

Additional Lyrics

2. Spider Murphy played the tenor saxophone,
   Little Joe was blowin' on the slide trombone.
   The drummer boy from Illinois went crash, boom, bang;
   The whole rhythm section was the Purple Gang.

3. Number Forty-seven said to number Three:
   "You're the cutest jailbird I ever did see.
   I sure would be delighted with your company,
   Come on and do the Jailhouse Rock with me."

4. The sad sack was a-sittin' on a block of stone,
   Way over in the corner weeping all alone.
   The warden said: "Hey, Buddy, don't you be no square,
   If you can't find a partner, use a wooden chair!"

5. Shifty Henry said to Bugs: "For heaven's sake,
   No one's lookin', now's our chance to make a break."
   Bugsy turned to Shifty and he said: "Nix, nix;
   I wanna stick around a while and get my kicks."

Jesu, Joy of Man's Desiring

By Johann Sebastian Bach

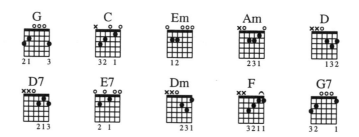

Strum Pattern: 8
Pick Pattern: 8

Intro
Moderately

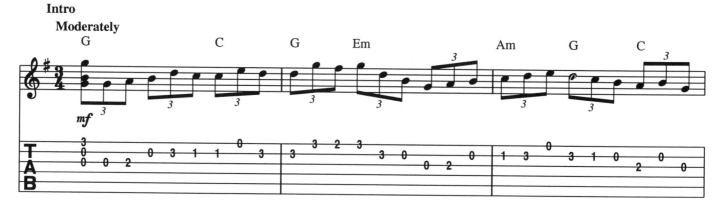

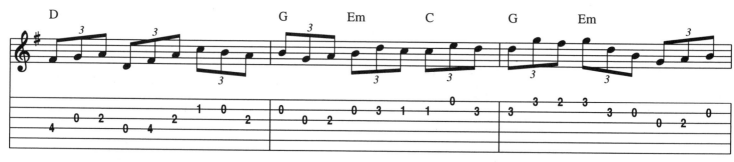

Verse

1. Je - su, joy of
2. *See Additional Lyrics*

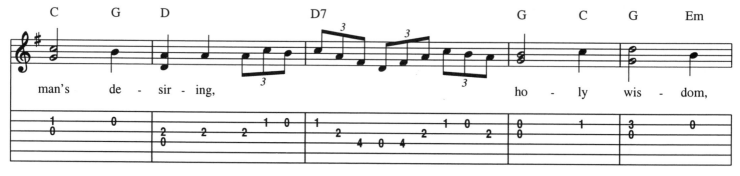

man's de - sir - ing,   ho - ly wis - dom,

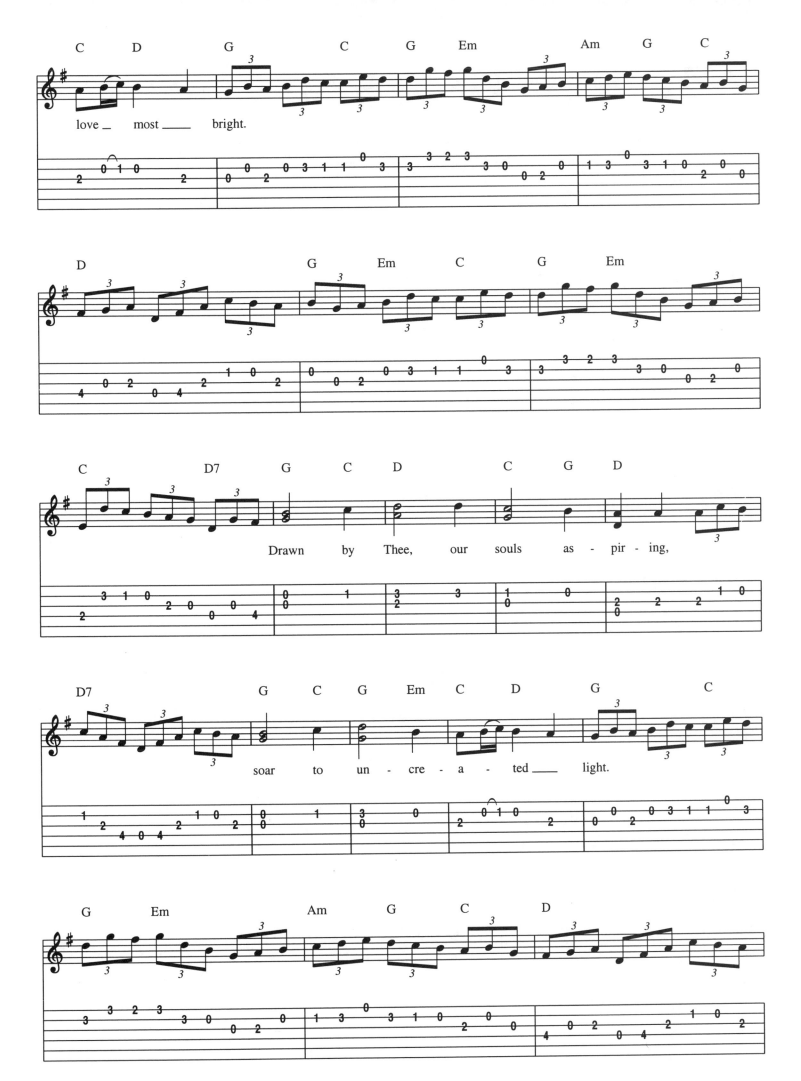

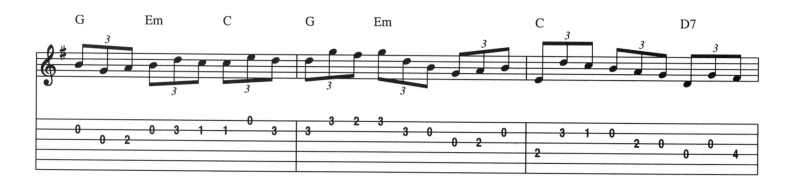

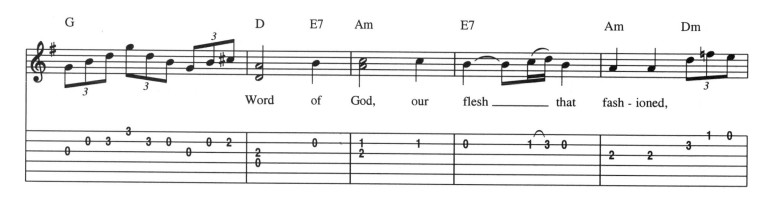

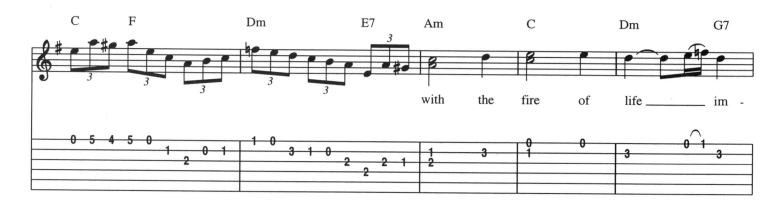

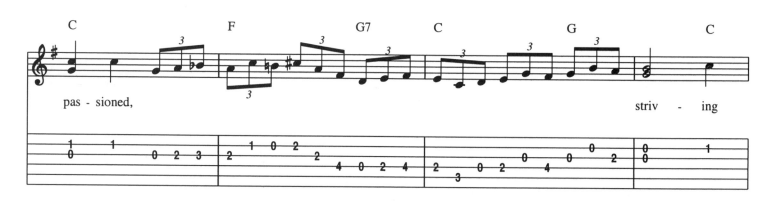

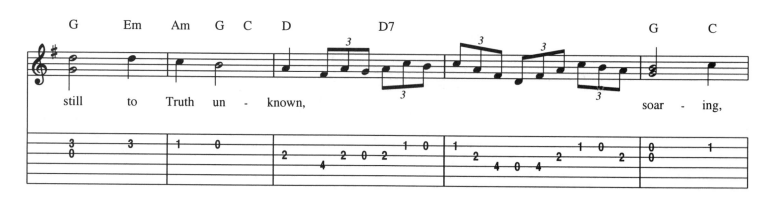

dy - ing   round ____ Thy _____ throne.

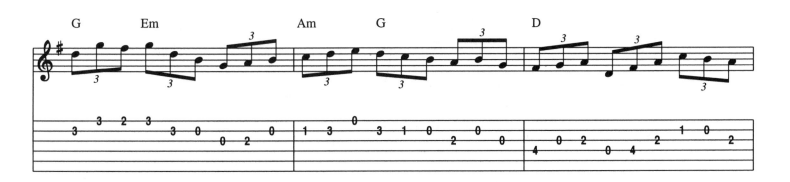

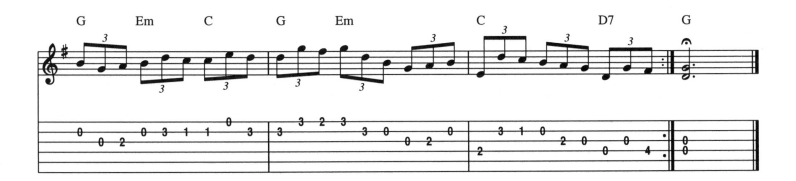

Additional Lyrics

2. Through the way where hope is guiding,
Hark, what peaceful music rings!
Where the flock in Thee confiding,
Drink of joy from deathless springs.
Their's is beauty's fairest pleasure,
Their's is wisdom's holiest treasure.
Thou dost ever lead Thine own,
In the love of joys unknown.

Just the Way You Are

Words and Music by Billy Joel

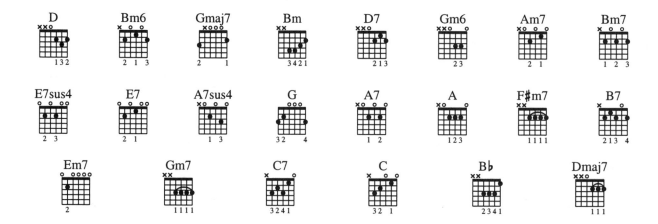

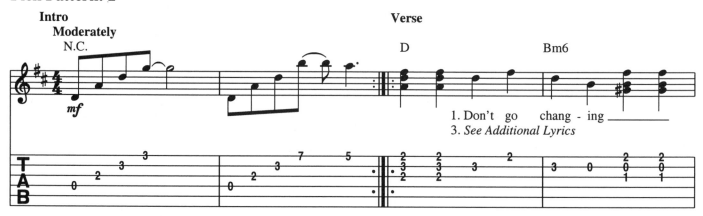

Strum Pattern: 1
Pick Pattern: 2

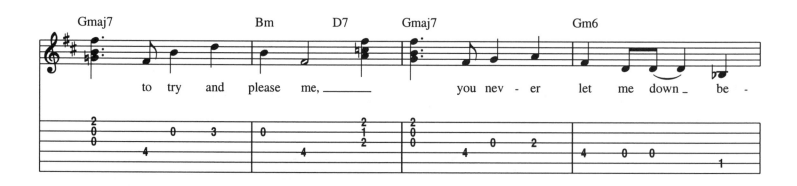

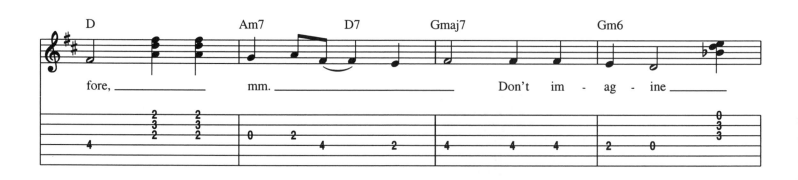

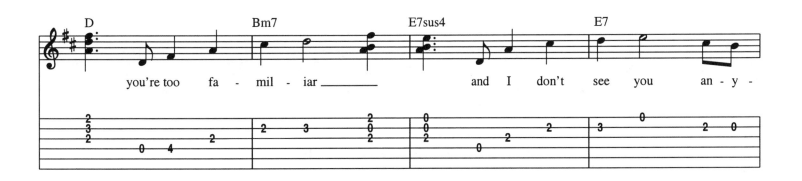

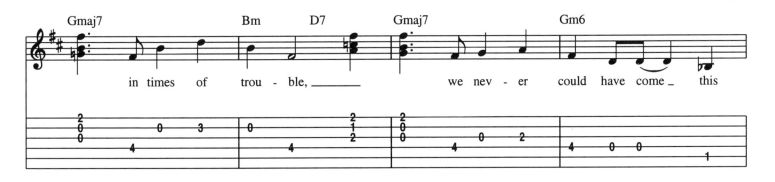

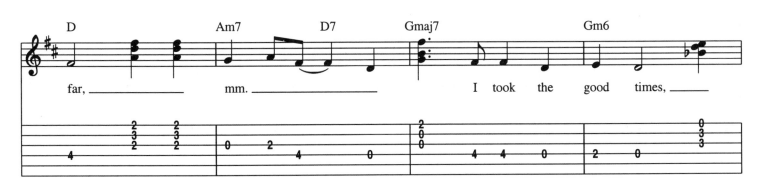

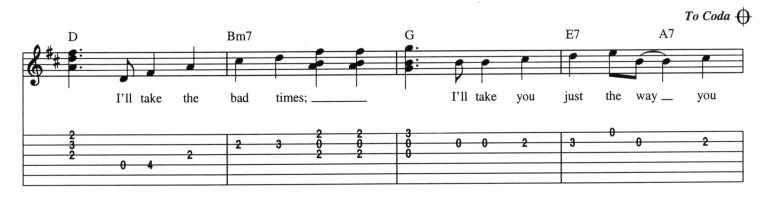

are.

Bridge

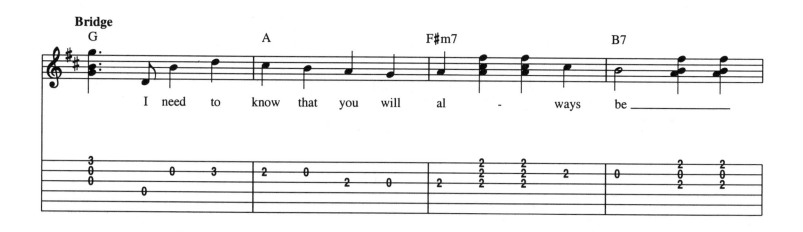

I need to know that you will al - ways be _____

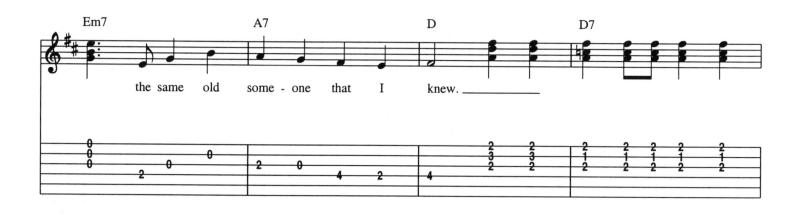

the same old some - one that I knew. _____

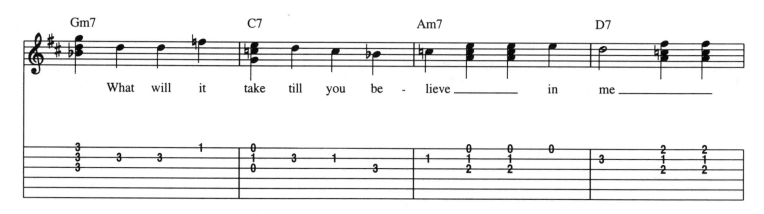

What will it take till you be - lieve _____ in me _____

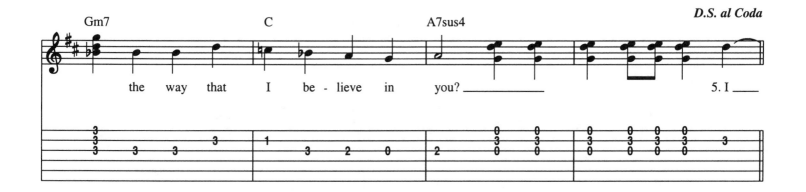

Gm7　　　　　　　　C　　　　　　　　A7sus4

the　way　that　I　be - lieve　in　you? _____　　　　　　5. I ___

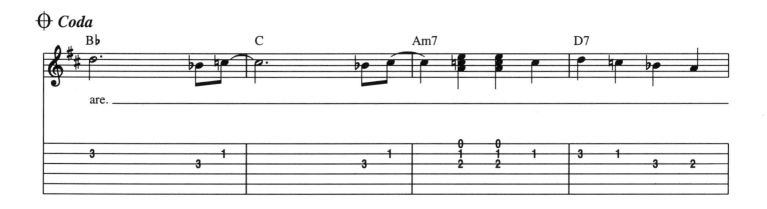

☩ *Coda*

B♭　　　　　　　C　　　　　　　Am7　　　　　　　D7

are. ___

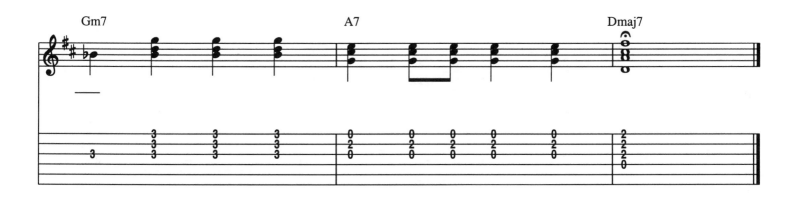

Gm7　　　　　　　　　　　A7　　　　　　　　Dmaj7

___

Additional Lyrics

3. Don't go trying some new fashion,
   Don't change the color of your hair, mm.
   You always have my unspoken passion,
   Although I might not seem to care.

4. I don't want clever conversation,
   I never want to work that hard, mm.
   I just want someone that I can talk to;
   I want you just the way you are.

5. I said I love you and that's forever,
   And this I promise from the heart, mm.
   I could not love you any better,
   I love you just the way you are.

Misty

Words by Johnny Burke
Music by Erroll Garner

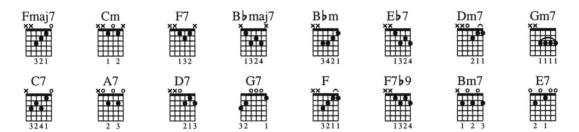

Strum Pattern: 4
Pick Pattern: 1

Verse
Slowly, With Expression

1. Look at me, _____ I'm as help-less as a kit-ten up a
2., 3. *See Additional Lyrics*

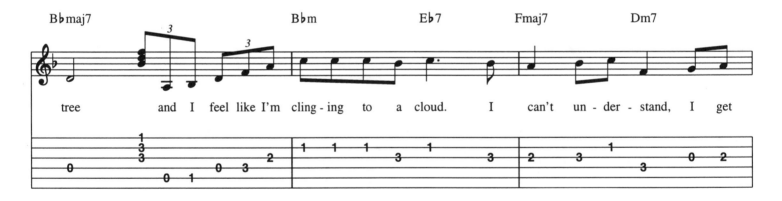

tree and I feel like I'm cling-ing to a cloud. I can't un-der-stand, I get

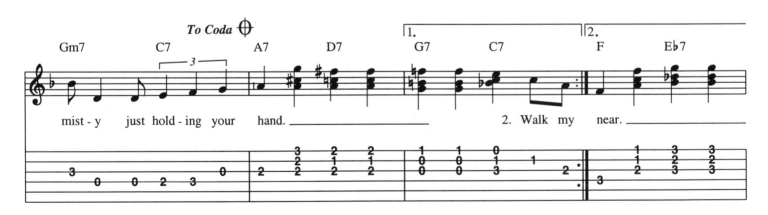

mist-y just hold-ing your hand. _____ 2. Walk my near. _____

110

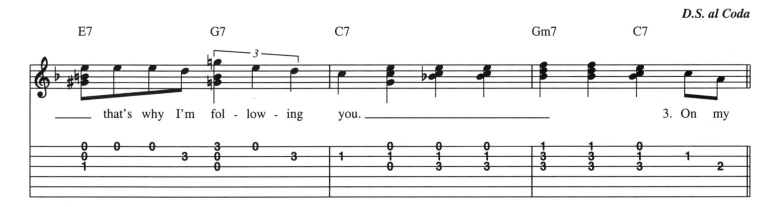

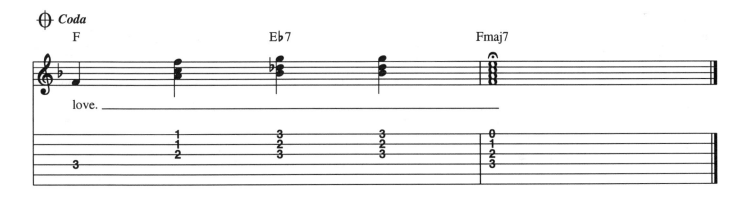

Additional Lyrics

2. Walk my way and a thousand violins begin to play,
    Or it might be the sound of your hello.
    That music I hear, I get misty,
    The moment you're near.

3. On my own, would I wander through this wonderland alone,
    Never knowing my right foot from my left,
    My hat from my glove?
    I'm too misty and too much in love.

Oh, Pretty Woman

Words and Music by Roy Orbison and Bill Dees

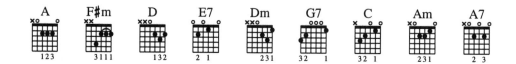

Strum Pattern: 2
Pick Pattern: 4

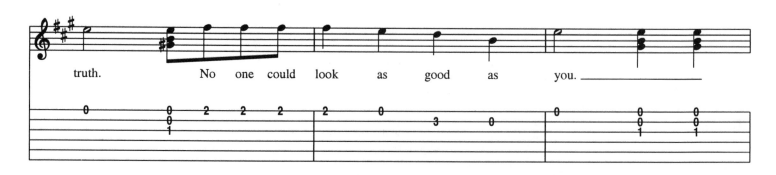

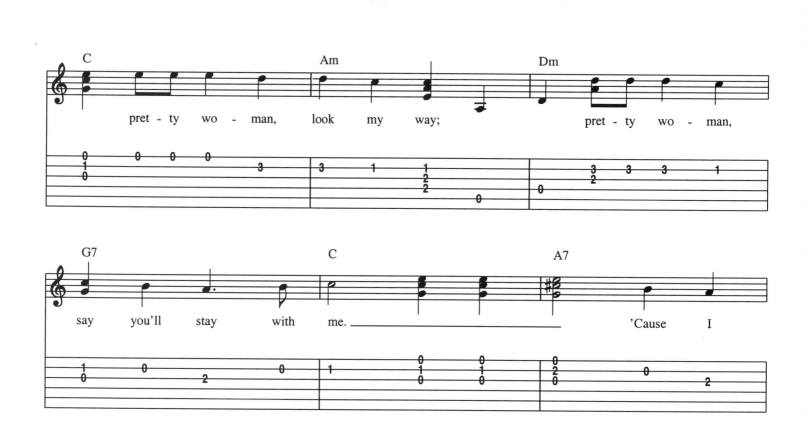

pret - ty wo - man, look my way; pret - ty wo - man,

say you'll stay with me. _____ 'Cause I

need you, _____ I'll treat you right. _____ Come to me

ba - by, _____ be mine to - night. _____

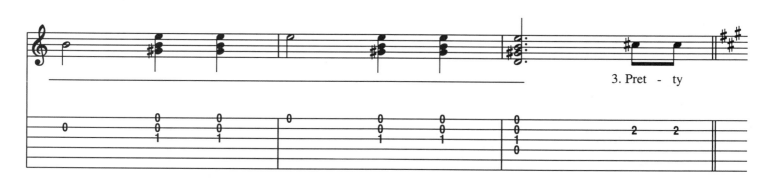

3. Pret - ty

114

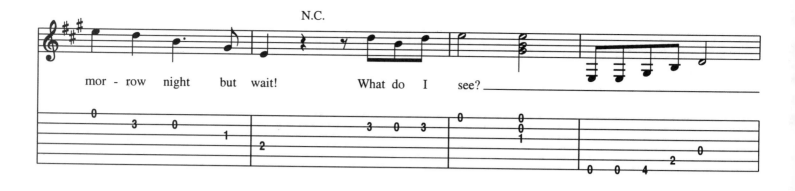

mor - row night but wait! What do I see?

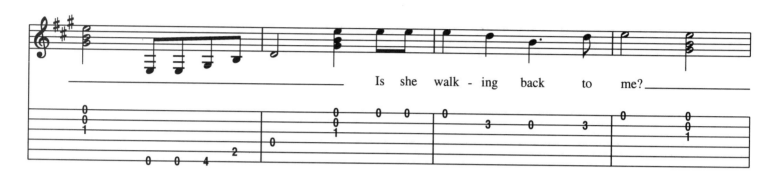

Is she walk - ing back to me?

Yeah, she's walk - ing back to me!

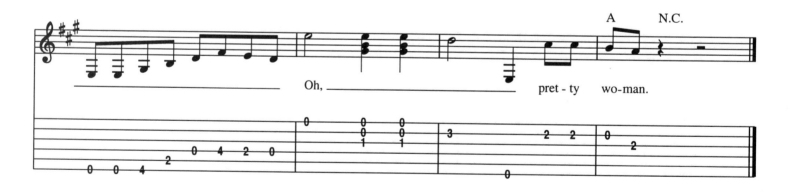

Oh, pret - ty wo-man.

Additional Lyrics

2. Pretty woman, won't you pardon me?
Pretty woman, I couldn't help but see;
Pretty woman, that you look lovely as can be.
Are you lonely just like me?

From a Distance

Words and Music by Julie Gold

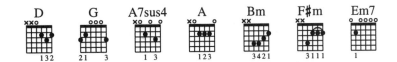

Strum Pattern: 2, 4
Pick Pattern: 1, 2

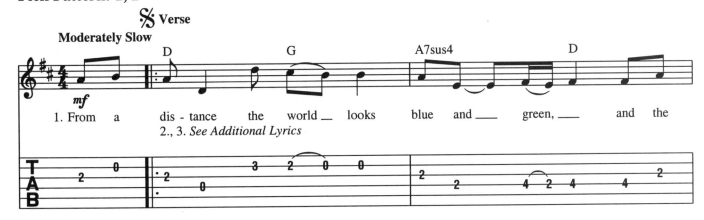

Verse

Moderately Slow

mf

1. From a dis - tance the world __ looks blue and __ green, __ and the
2., 3. *See Additional Lyrics*

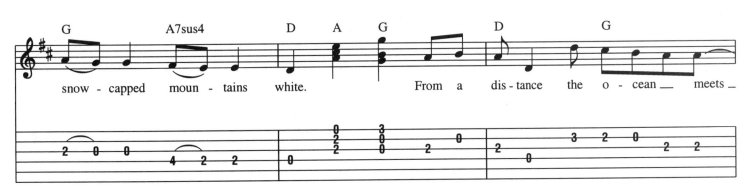

snow - capped moun - tains white. From a dis - tance the o - cean __ meets __

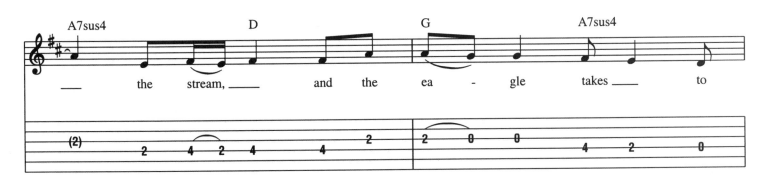

__ the stream, __ and the ea - gle takes __ to

flight. From __ a dis - tance there __ is har -

To Coda

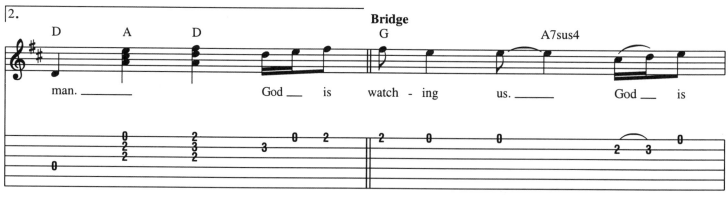

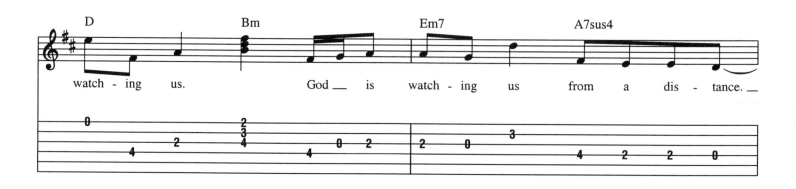

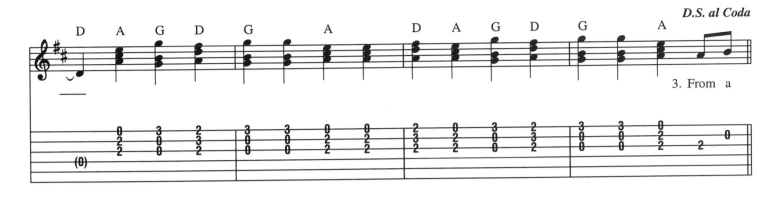

3. From a

⊕ *Coda*

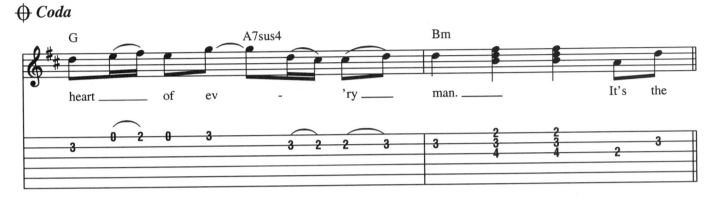

heart _____ of ev - 'ry _____ man. _____ It's the

Outro

hope of hopes, _____ it's the love of loves, _____ it's the

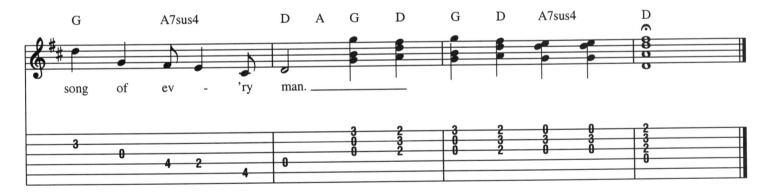

song of ev - 'ry man. _____

Additional Lyrics

2. From a distance we all have enough, and no one is in need.
   There are no guns, no bombs, no diseases, no hungry mouths to feed.
   From a distance we are instruments, marching in a common band.
   Playing songs of hope, playing songs of peace, they're the songs of ev'ry man.

3. From a distance you look like my friend, even though we are at war.
   From a distance I can't comprehend what all this war is for.
   From a distance there is harmony, and it echoes through the land.
   It's the hope of hopes, it's the love of loves, it's the heart of ev'ry man.

Shake, Rattle and Roll

Words and Music by Charles Calhoun

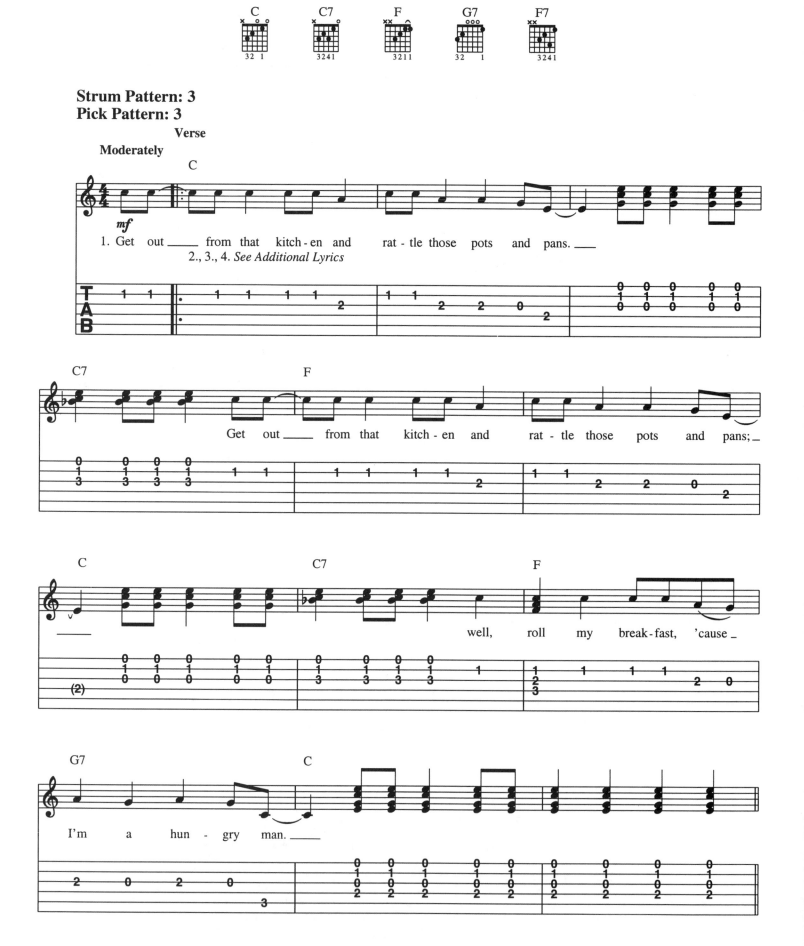

Chorus

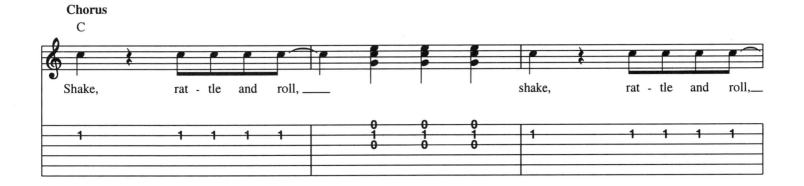

Shake, rat-tle and roll, _____ shake, rat-tle and roll, _____

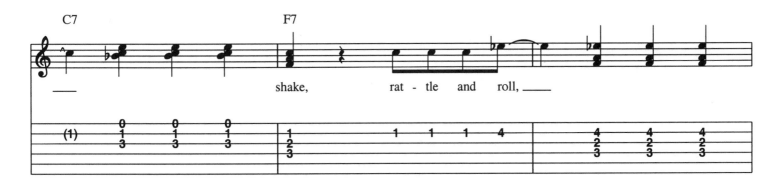

_____ shake, rat-tle and roll, _____

shake, rat-tle and roll, _____ you nev-er do noth-in' to save your dog-gone

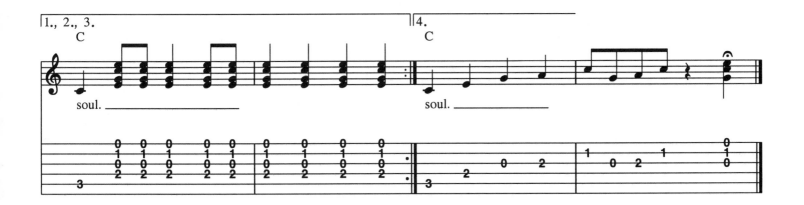

soul. _____ soul. _____

Additional Lyrics

2. Wearin' those dresses, your hair done up so right.
   Wearin' those dresses, your hair done up so right;
   You look so warm, but your heart is cold as ice.

3. I'm like a one-eyed cat, peepin' in a seafood store.
   I'm like a one-eyed cat, peepin' in a seafood store;
   I can look at you, tell you don't love me no more.

4. I believe you're doing me wrong and now I know.
   I believe you're doing me wrong and now I know;
   The more I work, the faster my money goes.

Torn

Words and Music by Phil Thornalley, Anne Previn and Scott Cutler

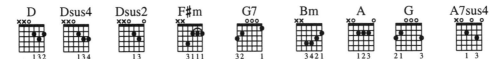

Strum Pattern: 2
Pick Pattern: 4

1. I thought I saw ___ a man brought ___ to life.
2. *See Additional Lyrics*

He was warm, ___ he came a - round ___ like he was

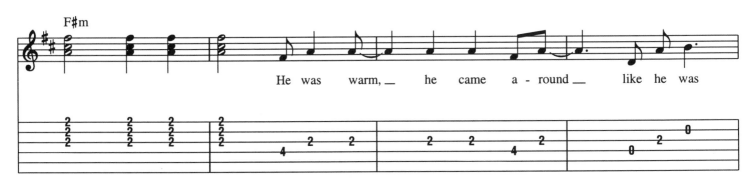

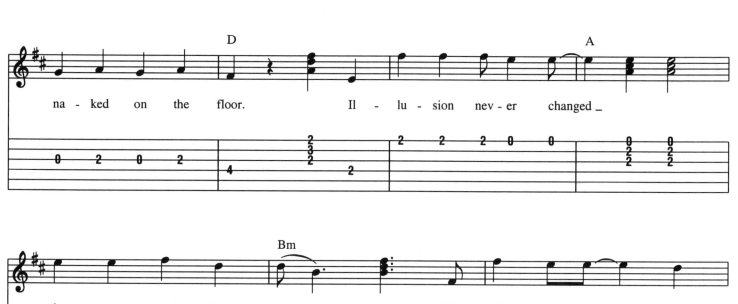

na - ked on the floor. Il - lu - sion nev - er changed ___

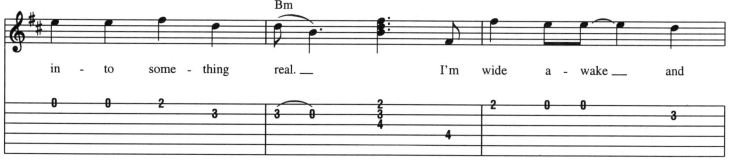

in - to some - thing real. ___ I'm wide a - wake ___ and

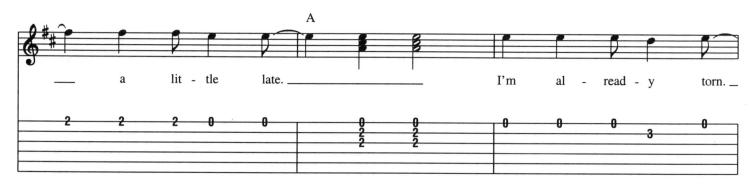

I can see the per - fect sky is torn. You're ___

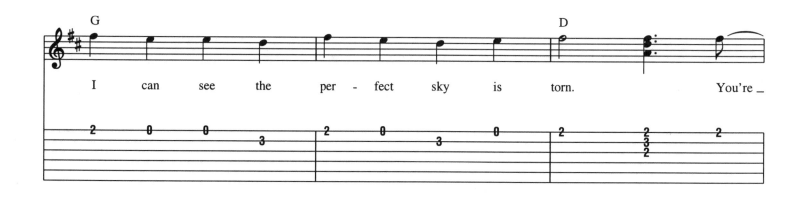

___ a lit - tle late. _____ I'm al - read - y torn. ___

To Coda ⊕

D.S. al Coda
(take 2nd ending)

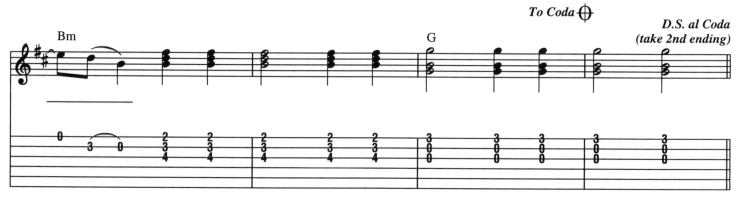

Chorus

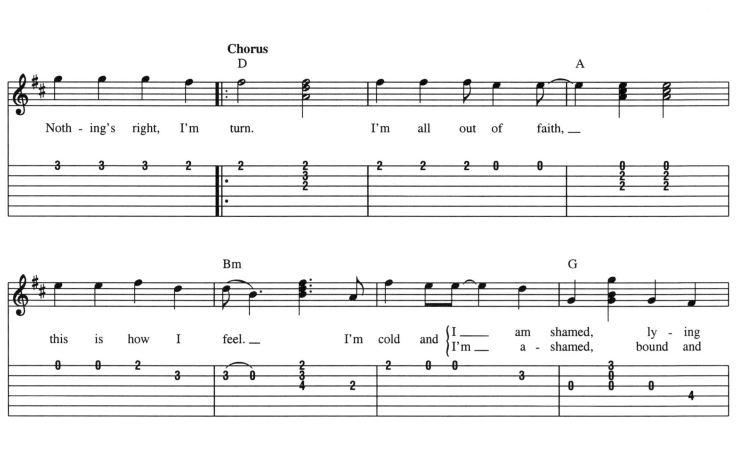

Noth - ing's right, I'm turn. I'm all out of faith, ___ this is how I feel. ___ I'm cold and {I ___ am shamed, ly - ing / I'm ___ a - shamed, bound and

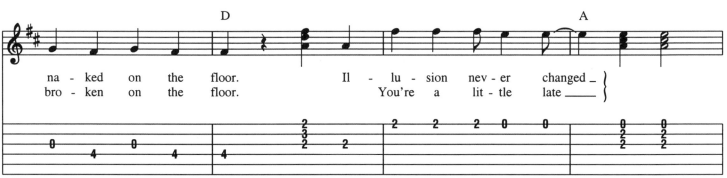

na - ked on the floor. Il - lu - sion nev - er changed ___ }
bro - ken on the floor. You're a lit - tle late ___ }

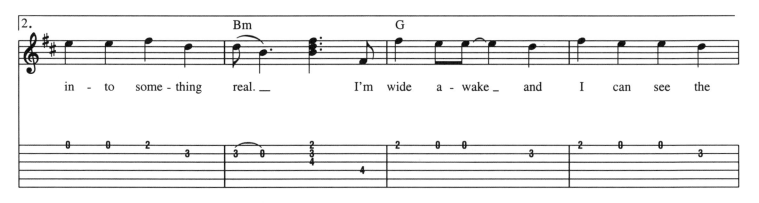

in - to some - thing real. ___ I'm wide a - wake ___ and I can see the

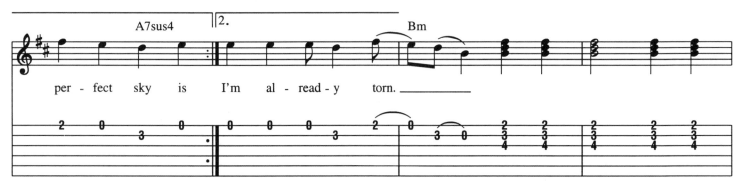

per - fect sky is I'm al - read - y torn. _____

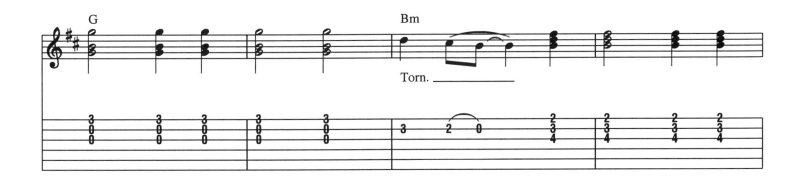

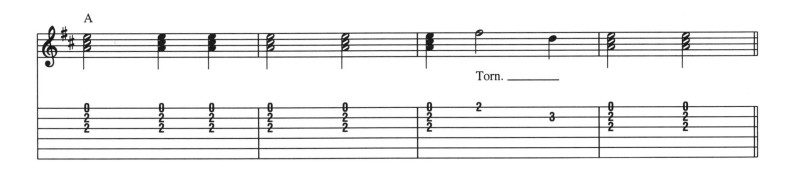

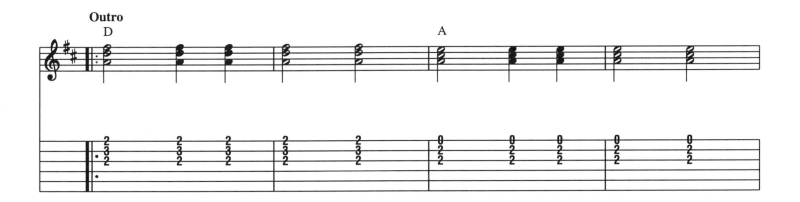

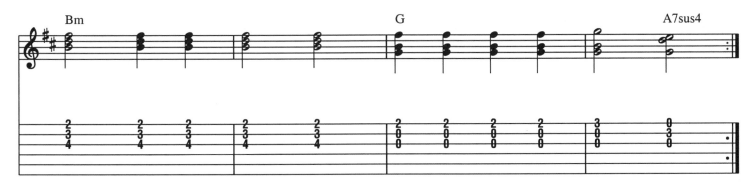

Additional Lyrics

2. Well, you couldn't be that man I adored.
   You don't seem to know or seem to care
   What your heart is for.
   Well, I don't know him anymore.

3. So, I guess the fortune teller's right.
   I should've seen just what was there
   And not some holy light.
   But you crawled beneath my veins and now...

Pre-Chorus I don't care, I have no luck.
   I don't miss it all that much.
   There's just so many things that I can't touch.

Twist and Shout

Words and Music by Bert Russell and Phil Medley

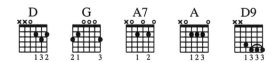

Strum Pattern: 6
Pick Pattern: 6

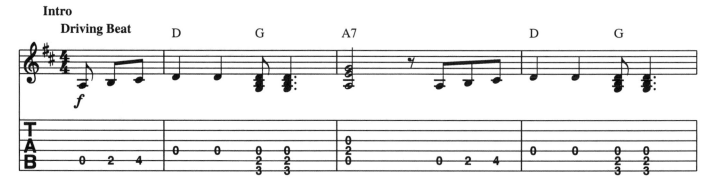

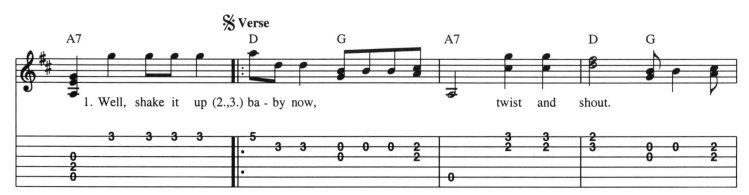

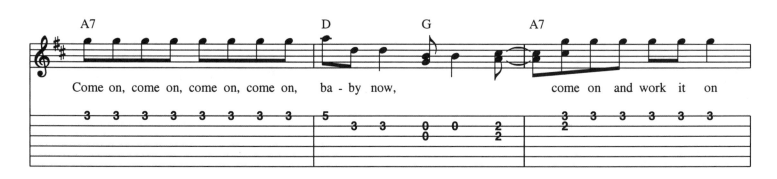

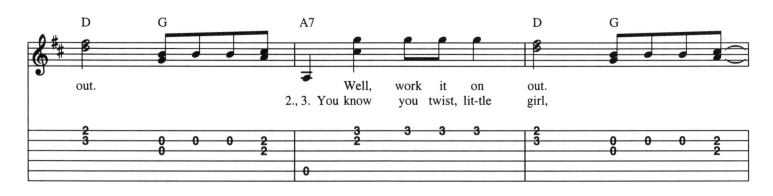

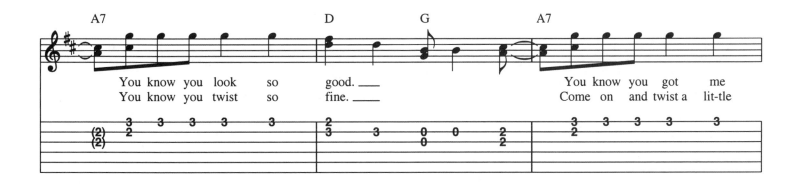

You know you look   so   good. ___
You know you twist   so   fine. ___
                                         You know you got   me
                                         Come on   and twist a lit-tle

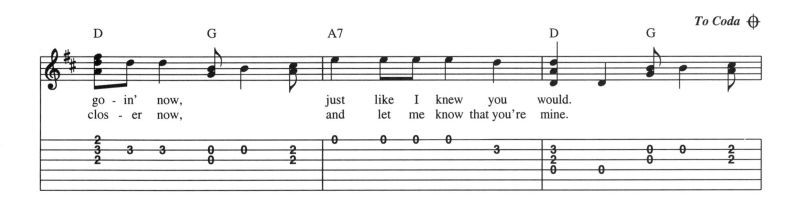

To Coda ⊕

go - in'   now,   just   like   I knew   you   would.
clos - er   now,   and   let   me know that you're   mine.

Guitar Solo   *play 4 times*

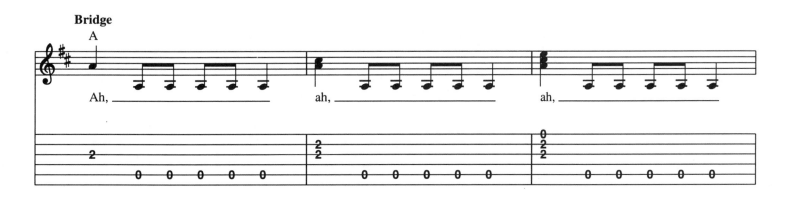

1.   ‖2.
2. Well, shake it   up   Oo.

Bridge

A

Ah, _____   ah, _____   ah, _____

129

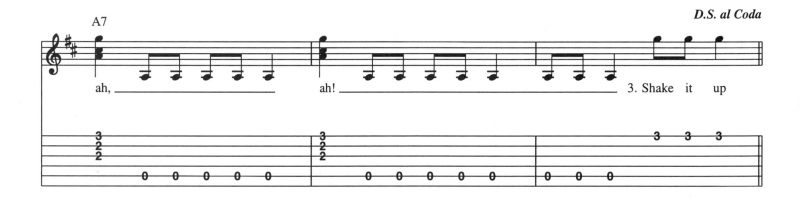

ah, _____ ah! _____ 3. Shake it up

⊕ *Coda*

Well, shake it, shake it, shake it, ba - by, now. Well, shake it, shake it, shake it,

ba - by, now. Ah, _____ ah, _____

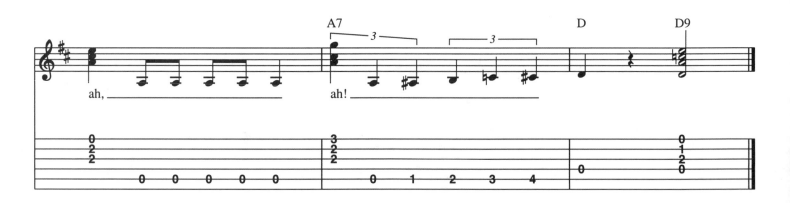

ah, _____ ah! _____

Wake Up Little Susie

Words and Music by Boudleaux Bryant and Felice Bryant

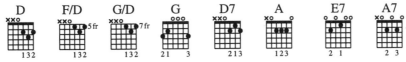

Strum Pattern: 1
Pick Pattern: 1

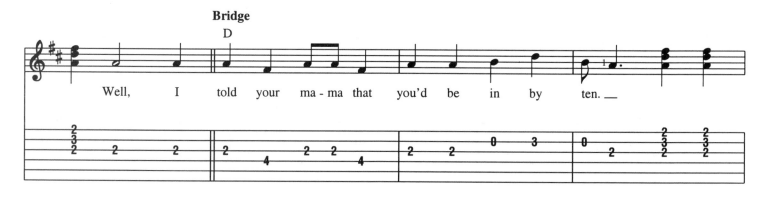

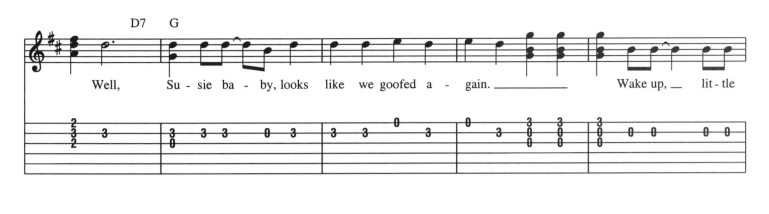

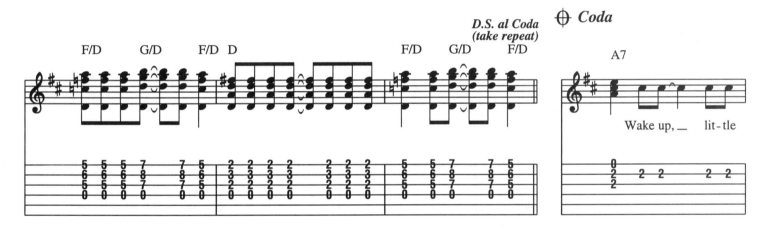

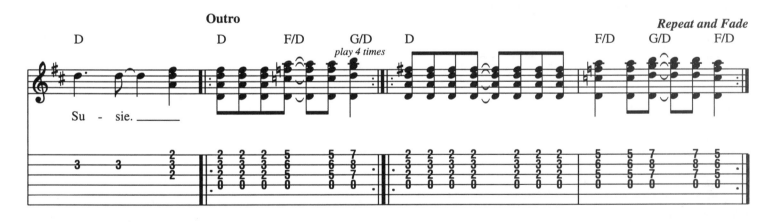

Additional Lyrics

3. The movie wasn't so hot.
   It didn't have much of a plot.
   We fell asleep, our goose is cooked,
   Our reputation is shot.
   Wake up, little Susie.
   Wake up, little Susie.

Walk This Way

Words and Music by Steven Tyler and Joe Perry

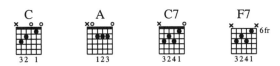

Strum Pattern: 3, 5
Pick Pattern: 3, 5

Intro
Lively
N.C.

Verse
C

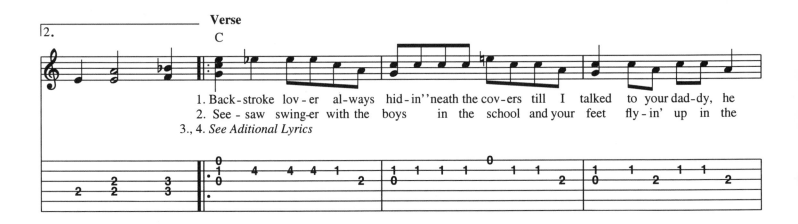

1. Back-stroke lov-er al-ways hid-in' 'neath the cov-ers till I talked to your dad-dy, he
2. See-saw swing-er with the boys in the school and your feet fly-in' up in the
3., 4. *See Aditional Lyrics*

say, he said, "You ain't seen noth-in' till you're down on a muf-fin, then you're
air, sing-in', "Hey, did-dle, did-dle," with your kit-ty in the mid-dle of the

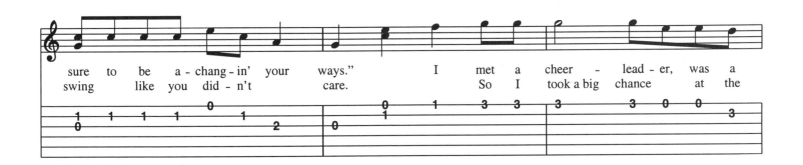

sure to be a - chang - in' your ways." I met a cheer - lead - er, was a
swing like you did - n't care. So I took a big chance at the

real young bleed - er, oh, the times I could rem - i - nisce; 'cause the
high school dance with a miss - y who was read - y to play. Was it

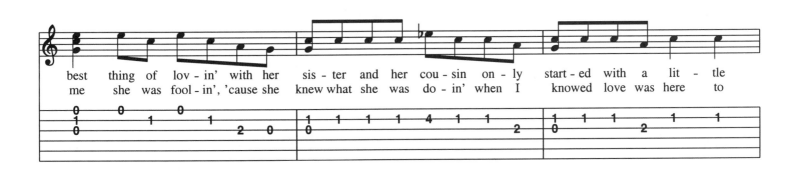

best thing of lov - in' with her sis - ter and her cou - sin on - ly start - ed with a lit - tle
me she was fool - in', 'cause she knew what she was do - in' when I knowed love was here to

1., 3.   A   N.C.

kiss *like this.*

stay *when she told me to*
She told me to
Walk this way, talk this way,

and just gim-me a kiss like this!

Additional Lyrics

3. School girl sweeties with a classy, kind-a sassy
Little skirts climbin' way up their knee.
There was three young ladies in the school gym locker
When I noticed they was lookin' at me.
I was a high school loser, never made it with a lady
Till the boys told me somethin' I missed.
Then my next door neighbor with a daughter had a favor,
So I gave her a little kiss like this.

4. See-saw swinger with the boys in the school
And your feet flyin' up in the air,
Singin' "Hey diddle, diddle." with your kitty in the middle
Of the swing like you didn't care.
So I took a big chance at the high school dance
With a missy who was ready to play.
Was it me she was foolin', cause she knew what she was doin'
When she told me how to walk this way.

What Would You Say

Words and Music by David J. Matthews

Strum Pattern: 2
Pick Pattern: 4

Verse

Moderate Rock

1. Up and down the pup-pies' hair ___ fleas and ticks ___ jump ev-
2., 4. *See Additional Lyrics*

'ry-where. ('Cause of o-rig - i-nal sin. ___) Down the hill fell Jack and Jill,

and you came tumb-bling ___ af-ter. ('Cause of o-rig - i-nal sin ___)

*Pre-Chorus

1. Rip a - way the tears, ___ drink a hope to
2., 3. *See Additional Lyrics*

*Use pattern 9 for ¾.

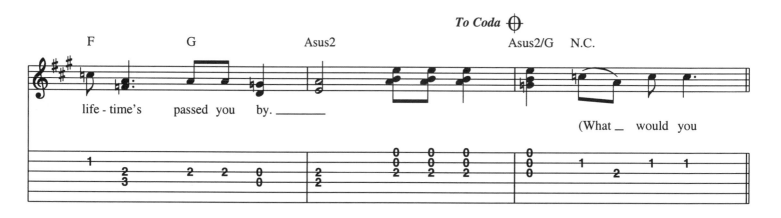

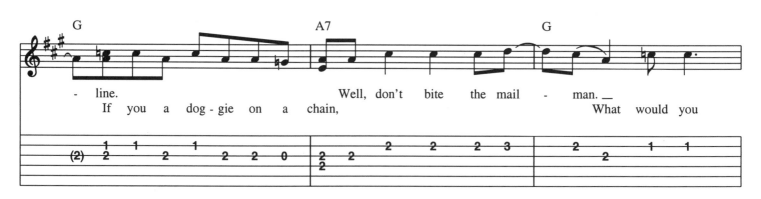

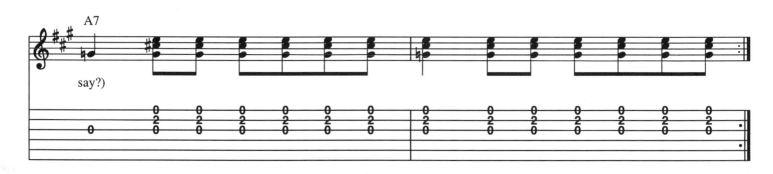

Verse

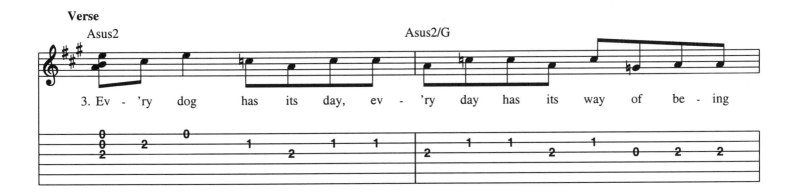

3. Ev - 'ry dog has its day, ev - 'ry day has its way of be - ing

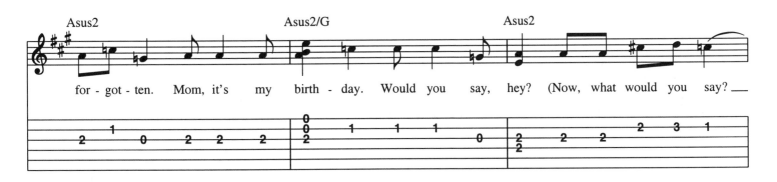

for - got - ten. Mom, it's my birth - day. Would you say, hey? (Now, what would you say? __

D.C. al Coda

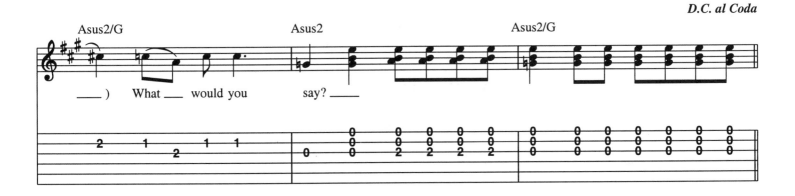

__) What __ would you say? __

✦ *Coda*

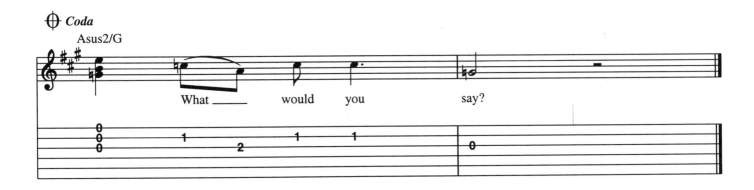

What ____ would you say?

Additional Lyrics

2., 4. I was there when the bear ate his head, thought it was candy.
(Everyone goes in the end.)
Knock, knock on the door. Who's it for? There's nobody in here.
(Look in the mirror, my friend.)

Pre-Chorus 2., 3. I don't understand, at best
And cannot speak for all the rest.
The morning will rise,
A lifetime's passed me by.

Where Do I Begin (Love Theme)

from the Paramount Picture LOVE STORY

Words by Carl Sigman • Music by Francis Lai

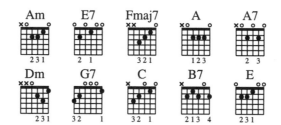

Strum Pattern: 4
Pick Pattern: 2

Verse
Moderately Slow

1. Where do I be-gin _____ to tell the sto-ry of how great a love can be; _____
2., 3. *See Additional Lyrics*

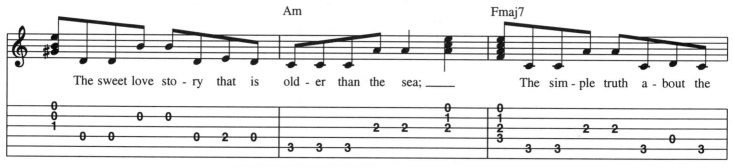

The sweet love sto-ry that is old-er than the sea; _____ The sim-ple truth a-bout the

To Coda ⊕

love she brings to me? _____ Where do I start? _____

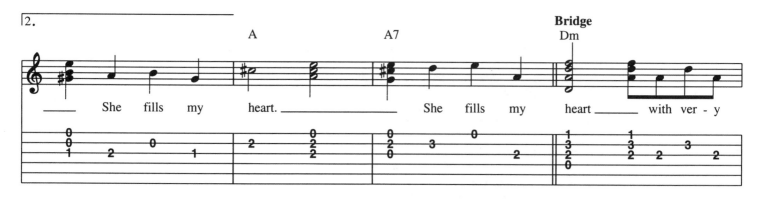

She fills my heart. _____ She fills my heart _____ with ver-y

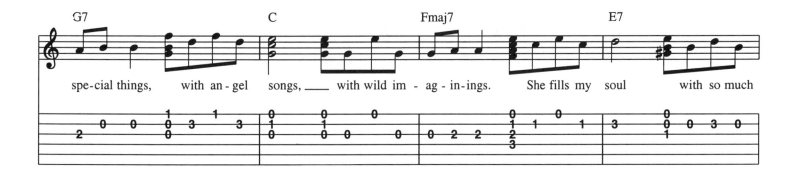

spe-cial things, with an-gel songs, ___ with wild im - ag - in-ings. She fills my soul with so much

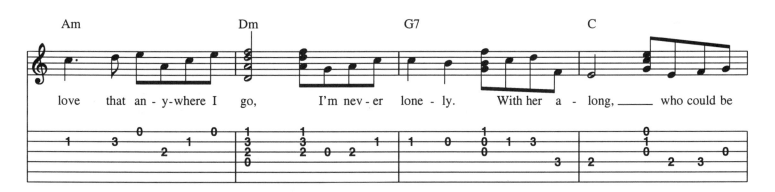

love that an - y-where I go, I'm nev - er lone - ly. With her a - long, ___ who could be

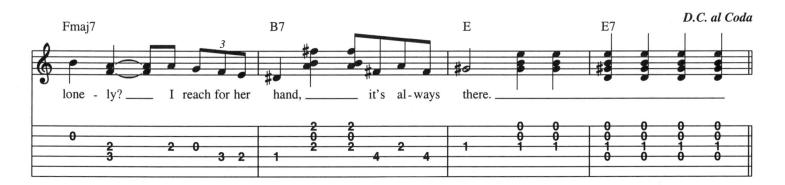

D.C. al Coda

lone - ly? ___ I reach for her hand, _____ it's al-ways there. _____

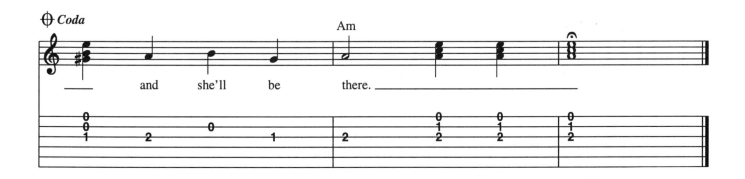

Coda

___ and she'll be there. _____

Additional Lyrics

2. With her first hello,
   She gave a meaning to this empty world of mine;
   There'd never be another love, another time;
   She came into my life and made the living fine.
   She fills my heart.

3. How long does it last?
   Can love be measured by the hours in a day?
   I have no answers now, but this much I can say;
   I know I'll need her till the stars all burn away,
   And she'll be there.

You Really Got Me

Words and Music by Ray Davies

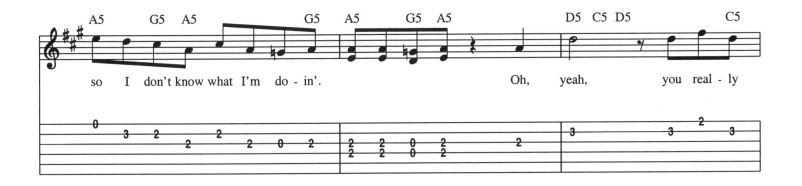

so I don't know what I'm do - in'. Oh, yeah, you real - ly

got me now. You got me so I can't sleep at night. You real - ly got me. You

real - ly got me. You real - ly got me.

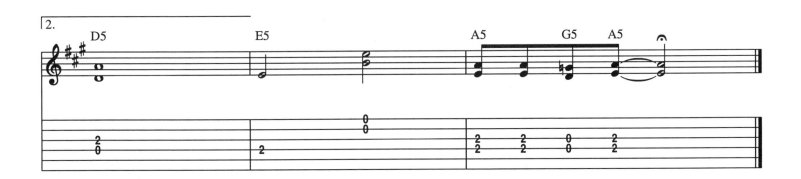

Additional Lyrics

2. See, don't ever set me free.
   I always want to be by your side.
   Yeah, you really got me now.
   You got me so I can't sleep at night.

You've Got a Friend

Words and Music by Carole King

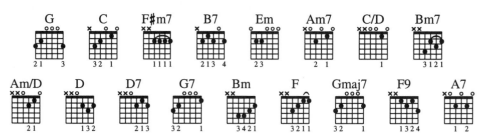

*Capo I

Strum Pattern: 3,4
Pick Pattern: 2,4

Intro

Slowly, With Expression

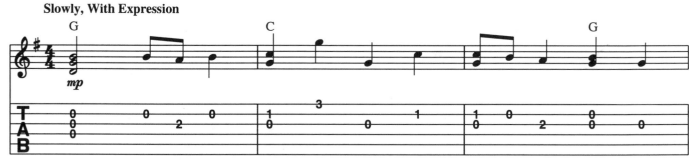

* Optional: To match recording, place capo at 1st fret.

Verse

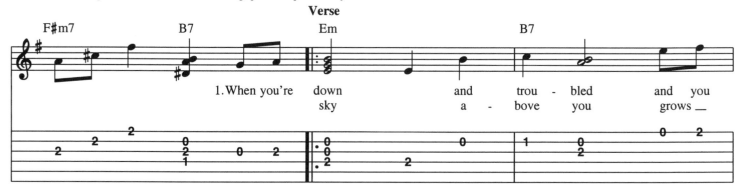

1. When you're down and trou-bled and you
   sky a - bove you grows —

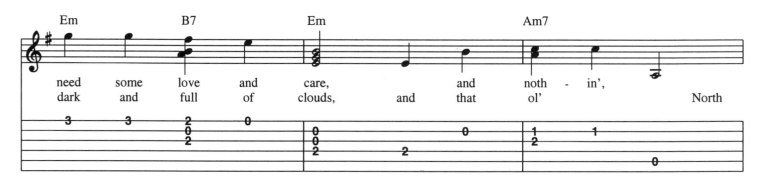

need some love and care, and noth-in',
dark some and full of clouds, and and that ol' North

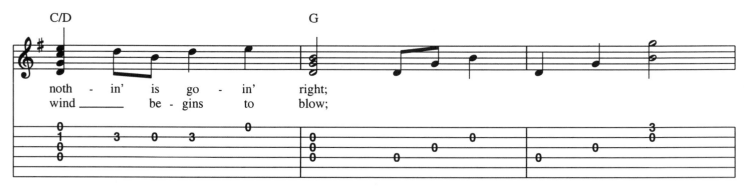

noth - in' is go - in' right;
wind _____ be - gins to blow;

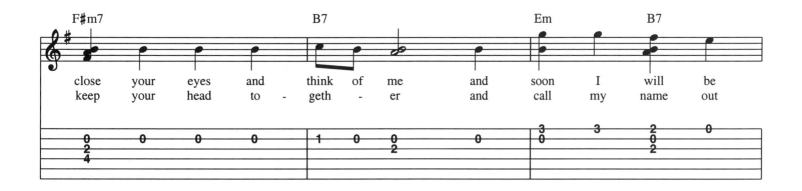

close your eyes and think of me and soon I will be
keep your head to - geth - er and soon call my name out

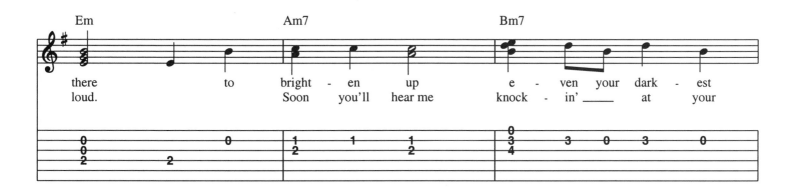

there to bright - en up e - ven your dark - est
loud. Soon you'll hear me knock - in' ____ at your

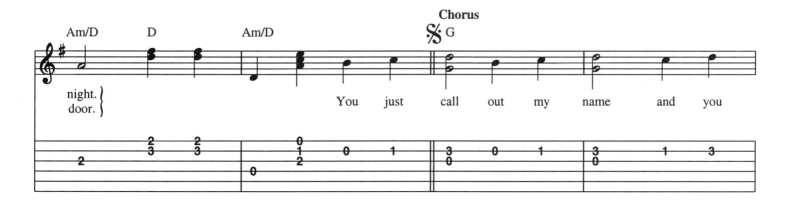

Chorus

night.
door.

You just call out my name and you

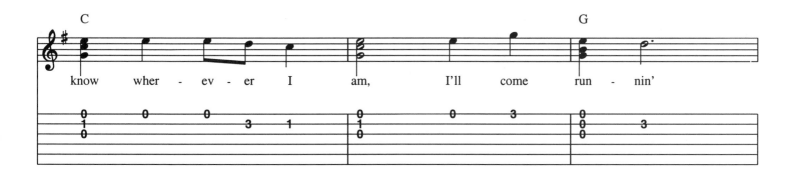

know wher - ev - er I am, I'll come run - nin'

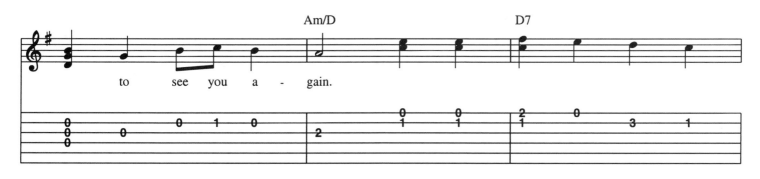

to see you a - gain.

Winter, spring, sum-mer or fall, ____ all you have to do is

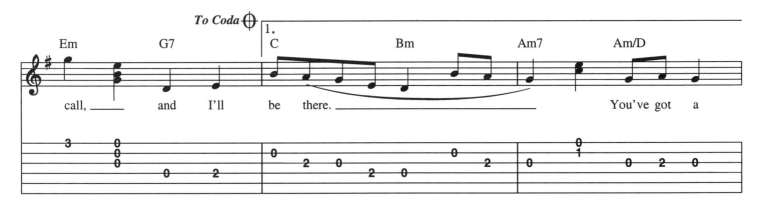

To Coda ⊕ | **1.**

call, ____ and I'll be there. _____ You've got a

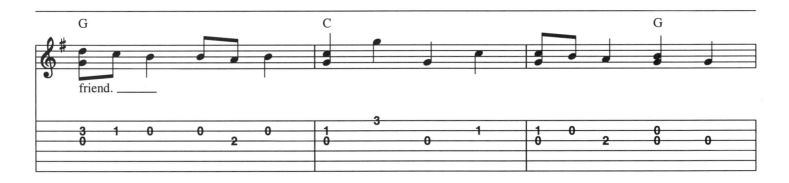

friend. _____

2.

2. If the be there, yes, I will. _____ Now

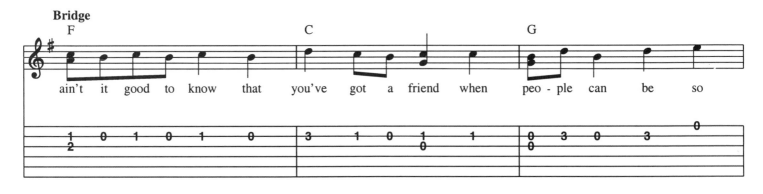

Bridge

ain't it good to know that you've got a friend when peo-ple can be so

cold? _____ They'll hurt you, yes, and de - sert you and

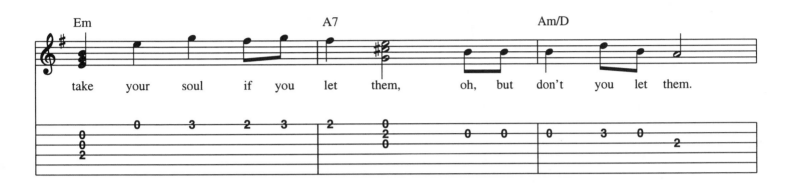

take your soul if you let them, oh, but don't you let them.

D.S. al Coda

You just

Coda

be there, ___ yes, I will. _____

___ You've got a friend. _____ You've got a

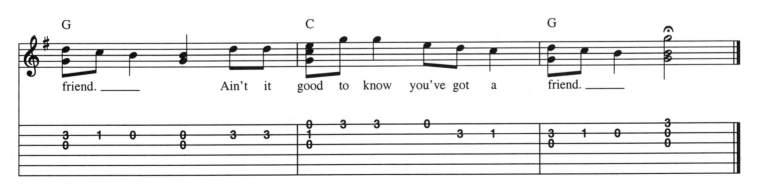

friend. _____ Ain't it good to know you've got a friend. _____

A Whole New World
(Aladdin's Theme)

from Walt Disney's ALADDIN
Music by Alan Menken
Lyrics by Tim Rice

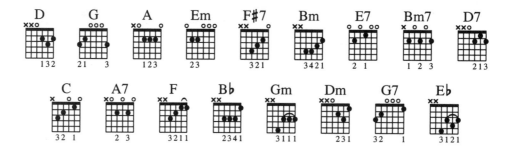

Strum Pattern: 4
Pick Pattern: 1

Verse
Moderately

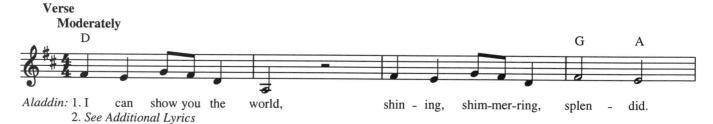

Aladdin: 1. I can show you the world, shin - ing, shim-mer-ring, splen - did.
2. *See Additional Lyrics*

Tell me prin-cess, now when did you last let your heart de - cide? ride. A whole new

Chorus

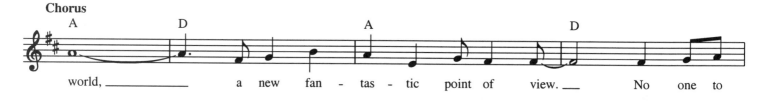

world, _____ a new fan - tas - tic point of view. __ No one to

tell us no, or where to go, or say we're on - ly dream - ing. *Jasmine:* A whole new

world, _____ a daz - zling place I nev - er knew. _ But, when I'm way up here, it's

crys - tal clear that now I'm in a whole new world with you.   *Jasmine:*
Aladdin: Now I'm in a whole new world with

Additional Lyrics

2. I can open your eyes,
   Take you wonder by wonder.
   Over, sideways and under
   On a magic carpet ride.

Another One Bites the Dust

Words and Music by John Deacon

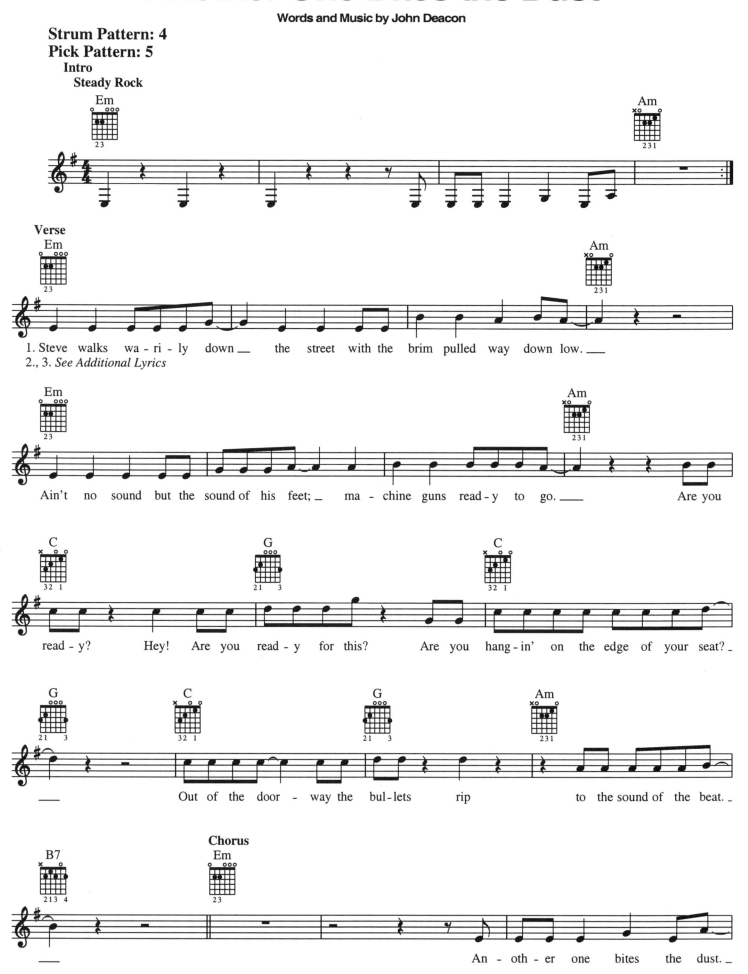

Additional Lyrics

2. How do you think I'm going to get along without you when you're gone?
   You took me for ev'rything that I had and kicked me out on my own.
   Are you happy? Are you satisfied?
   How long can you stand the heat?
   Out of the doorway the bullets rip to the sound of the beat.

3. There are plenty of ways can hurt a man and bring him to the ground.
   You can beat him. You can cheat him. You can treat him bad and leave him when he's down.
   But I'm ready, yes I'm ready for you.
   I'm standing on my own two feet.
   Out of the doorway the bullets rip, repeating to the sound of the beat.

Boot Scootin' Boogie

Words and Music by Ronnie Dunn

Strum Pattern: 1
Pick Pattern: 2

1. Out in the coun-try, past the cit-y lim-it sign, __ well, there's a hon-ky tonk __ near the
2., 3. *See Additional Lyrics*

coun-ty line. __ The joint starts jump-in' ev-'ry night when the sun __ goes

down. _____ They got whis-key, wom-en, _____

mu-sic and smoke. _ It's where all the cow-boy folk go to boot scoot-in'

1.
boo-gie. _____ 2. I've

2., 3.
Yeah, __
Whoa, __

Chorus

heel to toe, do-si-do, come on ba-by, let's go boot scoot-in'!

Woah, __ Cad - il - lac, black - jack, ba - by meet me out back, we're gon-na

boo-gie.

Oh, __ get down turn a - round, __ go to town, __ boot scoot-in'

To Coda ⊕ *D.C. al Coda* ⊕ *Coda*

boo - gie. __ 3. The

I __ said, get down, turn a - round, __

go to town, __ boot scoot-in' boo - gie. __ Whoa, __ get down, turn a - round, __

N.C.

go to town, __ boot scoot - in' boo - gie. __

Additional Lyrics

2. I've got a good job, I work hard for my money.
When it's quittin' time, I hit the door runnin'.
I fire up my pickup truck and let the horses run.
I go flyin' down that highway to that hideaway,
Stuck out in the woods, to do the boot scootin' boogie.

3. The bartender asks me, says, "Son, what will it be?"
I want a shot at that red-head yonder lookin' at me.
The dance floor's hoppin' and it's hotter than the Fourth of July.
I see outlaws, in laws, crooks and straights,
All makin' it shake doin' the boot scootin' boogie.

Don't Cry for Me Argentina

from EVITA
Words by Tim Rice
Music by Andrew Lloyd Webber

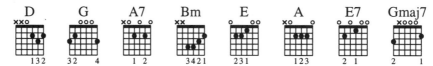

Strum Pattern: 1
Pick Pattern: 2

Verse
Slowly

1. It won't be eas-y, you'll think it's strange when I try to ex-plain how I
2., 3. *See Additional Lyrics*

feel.   That I still need your love af-ter all that I've done.   You won't be - lieve me.

All   you will see   is a girl you once knew,   al-though she's dressed up   to the nines   at

six - es and sev - ens with you.   Don't cry for me Ar-gen - ti - na.   The   truth is I nev - er

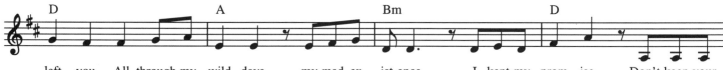

left   you. All through my wild days,   my mad ex - ist-ence,   I kept my prom - ise.   Don't keep your

To Coda ⊕ *D.C. al Coda*   ⊕ *Coda*

dis-tance.___   Have   I   said   too much? There's noth-ing more I can think of to

say to you,   but all you have to do is   look at me to know that ev-'ry word is   true. ___

Additional Lyrics

2. I had to let it happen, I had to change.
   Couldn't stay all my life down at heel,
   Looking out of the window, staying out of the sun,
   So I chose freedom.
   Running around trying ev'rything new,
   But nothing impressed me at all.
   I never expected it to.

3. And as for fortune and fame,
   I never invited them in.
   Thought it seemed to the world they were all I desired.
   They are illusions.
   They are not the solutions they promise to be.
   The answer was here all the time.
   I love you and hope you love me.

MCA Music Publishing

Heartache Tonight

Words and Music by John David Souther, Don Henley, Glenn Frey and Bob Seger

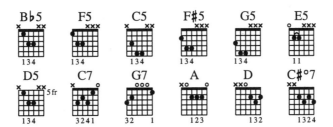

Strum Pattern: 3
Pick Pattern: 2, 3

Intro
Moderate Blues

1., 3. Some-bod-y's gon-na hurt some-one ___

be-fore the night is through. ___ Some-bod-y's gon-na come un - done; ___

there's noth-in' we can do. ___ Ev-'ry-bod-y wants to touch some-bod - y,

if it takes all night. ___ Ev-'ry-bod-y wants to take a lit-tle chance, ___

make it come out right. ___ There's gon-na be a heart-ache to-night, a

heart-ache to-night, I know. ___ There's gon-na be a heart-ache to-night, a

heart-ache to-night, I know. ___ Lord, I know. ___ 2. Some peo-ple like to

stay out   late. _   Some folks can't hold out that   long. _____   But no - bod - y wants to

go home   now; _   there's too much go - in'   on. _____

This night is gon - na   last for - ev -   er.   Last all, last all   sum - mer

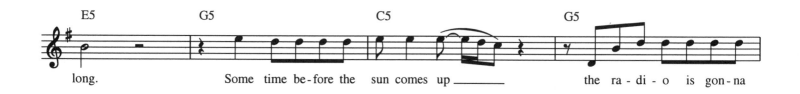

long.   Some time be - fore the   sun comes up _____   the ra - di - o   is gon - na

Chorus

play that   song. _____   There's gon - na be a   heart - ache to - night,   a

heart - ache to - night,   I know. _____   There's gon - na be a

heart - ache to - night,   a   heart ache to - night, I know. __   Lord, I

know. __   There's gon - na be a   heart - ache to - night,   the moon's shin - in' bright,   so

turn out the light, and we'll get it right.__ There's gon-na be a heart-ache to-night,__ a

heart-ache to-night, I know. __

⊕ *Coda*

__ Let's go. _____ We can

Outro

beat a-round the bush-es; we can get down to the bone; we can leave it in the park-in' lot, but

ei-ther way, there's gon-na be a heart-ache to-night,_____ a heart-ache to-night, I know.__

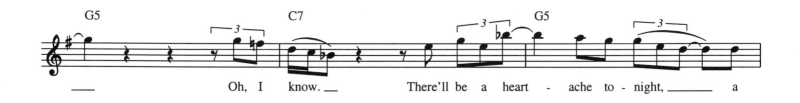

__ Oh, I know. __ There'll be a heart-ache to-night,_____ a

heart-ache to-night, I know. __

157

Have I Told You Lately

Words and Music by Van Morrison

Bm — Am7 — C/D — G — Am7 G7

and some-how you make it bet-ter, ease my trou-bles that's ___ what you do.

Bridge

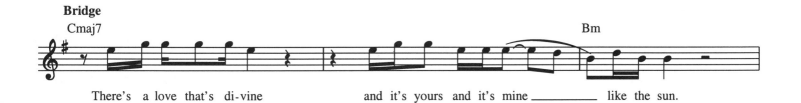

Cmaj7 — Bm

There's a love that's di-vine and it's yours and it's mine _____ like the sun.

Am7 Bm Cmaj7

And at the end of the day we should give thanks and pray _____

1.

2.

D.S. al Coda

Bm — C/D — C/D

to the one, __ to the one. __ Have I to the one. __ And have I

✛ *Coda*

G — Am7 G7 Cmaj7 — Bm

do. Take a-way all __ my sad-ness, fill my life with glad-ness,

Am7 — C/D — G — Am7 G7 Cmaj7

ease my trou-bles that's _ what you do. Take a-way all __ my sad-ness,

Bm — Am7 — C/D — G

fill my heart with glad-ness, ease my trou-bles that's _ what you do. _____

rit.

Hit Me With Your Best Shot

Words and Music by Eddie Schwartz

Strum Pattern: 3
Pick Pattern: 3

1. Well, you're a real tough cook-ie with a long his-to-ry of break-ing lit-tle hearts like the
2., 3. *See Additional Lyrics*

one in me. That's O. K. Let's see how you do it. Put up your dukes,_ let's get down to it.

Hit me with your best shot. Why don't you hit me with your best shot?_

Hit me with your best shot. Fire _ a - way. _____ 2. You

way.

Additional Lyrics

2. You come on with a come on.
   You don't fight fair.
   But that's O.K. See if I care.
   Knock me down. It's all in vain.
   I'll get right back on my feet again.

3. Well, you're a real tough cookie with a long history.
   Of breaking little hearts like the one in me.
   Before I put another notch in my lipstick case,
   You better make sure you put me in my place.

I Shot the Sheriff

Words and Music by Bob Marley

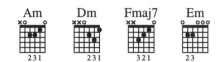

Strum Pattern: 3
Pick Pattern: 3

Additional Lyrics

2. Sheriff John Brown always hated me;
   For what, I don't know.
   And every time that I plant a seed,
   He said, "Kill it before it grows,"
   "Kill it before it grows."

3. Freedom came my way one day,
   So I started out of town.
   All of a sudden, I see Sheriff Brown
   Aimin' to shoot me down,
   So I shot him down.

4. Reflexes got the better of me,
   What will be will be.
   Everyday, the bucket goes to the well,
   One day the bottom will drop out
   I say, one day the bottom will drop out.

I Can't Help Myself (Sugar Pie, Honey Bunch)

Words and Music by Brian Holland, Lamont Dozier and Edward Holland

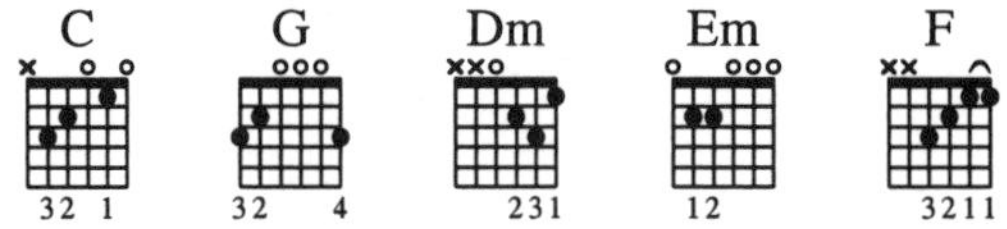

C G Dm Em F
32 1
32 4
231
12
3211

Strum Pattern: 3
Pick Pattern: 3

Intro
Moderately Fast

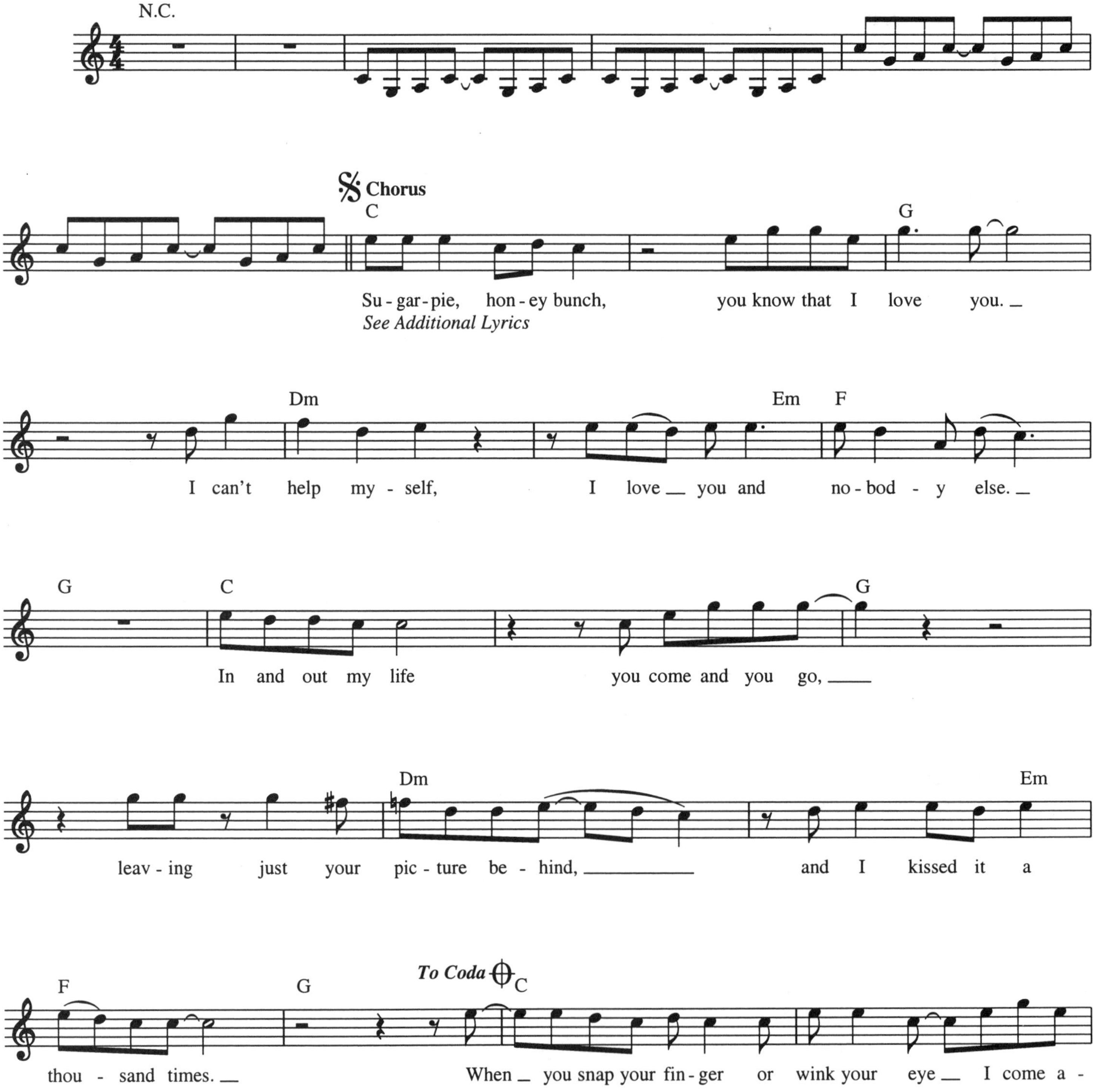

N.C.
Chorus
C
G
Su - gar - pie, hon - ey bunch, you know that I love you. _
See Additional Lyrics
Dm
Em F
I can't help my - self, I love _ you and no - bod - y else. _
G C G
In and out my life you come and you go, ___
Dm Em
leav - ing just your pic - ture be - hind, ______ and I kissed it a
To Coda
F G C
thou - sand times. _ When _ you snap your fin - ger or wink your eye _ I come a -

Additional Lyrics

Chorus Sugarpie, honey bunch, I'm weaker than a man should be.
I can't help myself, I'm a fool in love you see.
Wanna tell you I don't love you, tell you that we're through, and I've tried.
But ev'ry time I see your face I get all choked up inside.
When I call your name, girl,
It starts the flame burning in my heart,
Tearing it all apart.
No matter how I try, my love I cannot hide.

Jambalaya (On the Bayou)

Words and Music by Hank Williams

Strum Pattern: 3
Pick Pattern: 3

1. Good-bye, Joe, me got-ta go, me oh,
2., 3. *See Additional Lyrics*

my oh. ___ Me got-ta go pole the pi-rogue down the bay-ou. ___ My Y-

vonne, the sweet-est one, me oh, my oh. ___ Son of a gun, we'll have big fun on the

bay-ou. ___ Jam-ba-la-ya and a craw-fish pie and fil-let gum-bo, ___ 'cause to-

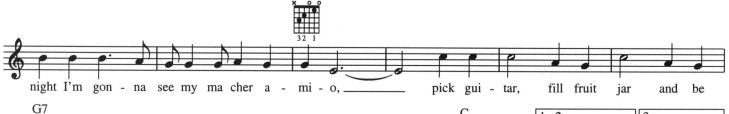

night I'm gon-na see my ma cher a-mi-o, ___ pick gui-tar, fill fruit jar and be

gay-o. ___ Son of a gun, we'll have big fun on the bay-ou. ___ 2. Thi-bo

Additional Lyrics

2. Thi bo daux, Fontaineaux, the place is buzzin'.
Kinfolk come to see Yvonne by the dozen.
Dress in style and go hog wild, me oh, my oh.

3. Settle down far from town, get me a pirogue,
And I'll catch all the fish in the bayou.
Swap my mon to buy Yvonne what we need-o.

Love Me Tender

Words and Music by Elvis Presley and Vera Matson

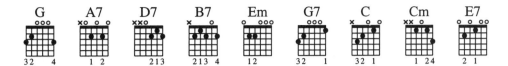

Strum Pattern: 4
Pick Pattern: 6

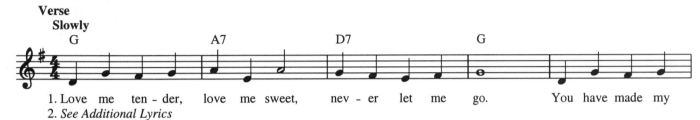

Verse
Slowly

1. Love me ten - der, love me sweet, nev - er let me go. You have made my
2. *See Additional Lyrics*

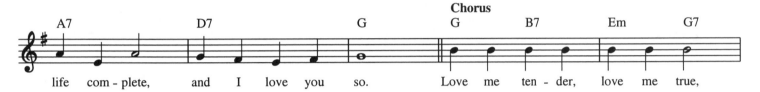

life com - plete, and I love you so. Love me ten - der, love me true,

Chorus

all my dreams ful - fill. For, my dar - lin', I love you, and I al - ways will.

Verse

3. Love me ten - der, love me dear, tell me you are mine. I'll be yours through

Outro-Chorus

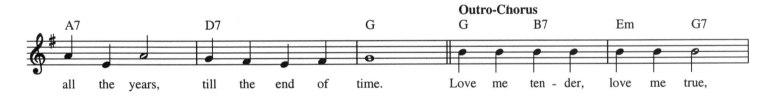

all the years, till the end of time. Love me ten - der, love me true,

all my dreams ful - fill. For, my dar - lin', I love you, and I al - ways will.

Additional Lyrics

2. Love me tender, love me long,
   Take me to your heart.
   For it's there that I belong,
   And we'll never part.

The Magic Bus

Words and Music by Peter Townshend

ba - by each day. Too much, the ma - gic bus! ___

Chorus

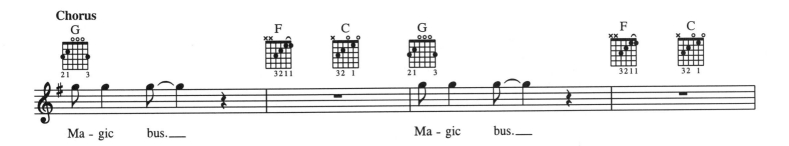

Ma - gic bus. ___ Ma - gic bus. ___

D.C. al Coda
(take repeat)

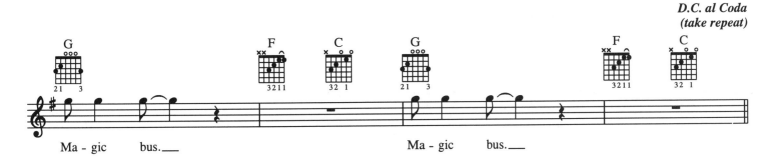

Ma - gic bus. ___ Ma - gic bus. ___

⊕ *Coda*
Outro

Repeat and Fade

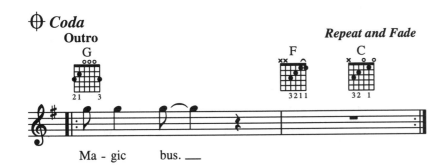

Ma - gic bus. ___

Additional Lyrics

2. Thank you, driver, for gettin' me here.
You'll be an inspector, have no fear.
I don't wanna cause no fuss,
But can I buy your magic bus?

4. Three pence and six pence everyday,
Just to drive to my baby.
Three pence and six pence each day;
Drive my baby every way.

5. Now I got my magic bus.
I said, "Now I got my magic bus."
I drive my baby every way.
Each time I go a different way.

6 Everyday you'll see the dust,
I drive my baby in the magic bus.

Miss You

Words and Music by Mick Jagger and Keith Richards

Am   Dm   F   Em   E

Strum Pattern: 1
Pick Pattern: 2

Verse
Moderately

1. I've been hold-ing out so long, I've been sleep-ing all a-lone, Lord I miss you.

I've been hang-ing on the phone, I've been sleep-ing all a-lone, I want to kiss you. Hoo, hoo,

Chorus

hoo, __ hoo, _____ hoo, hoo, hoo, _ hoo, _____ hoo, hoo, hoo, hoo. _ Hoo, hoo,

Verse

2. Well, I've been haunt-ed in my sleep, _ you've been star-ring in my dreams, Lord I

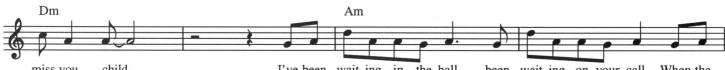

miss you child. _ I've been wait-ing in the hall, been wait-ing on your call. When the

phone rings, *Spoken:* It's just some friends of mine that say, "Hey, *what's the matter man? We're gonna come around at twelve o'clock*
gonna bring a case of wine, hey, let's go mess and fool around,

Chorus

with some Puerto Rican girls that are just dyin' to meet you. We're ha, ha, ha, _ ha, _____ ha, ha,
you know like we   used to."   Ha, ha,
*sung 2nd time

Bridge

ha, ha, ha, _ ha, _____ ha, ha, ha, ha. _   Ha, ha,   Oh!

My Favorite Things

from THE SOUND OF MUSIC
Lyrics by Oscar Hammerstein II
Music by Richard Rodgers

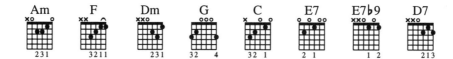

Strum Pattern: 7
Pick Pattern: 8

Verse
Moderately

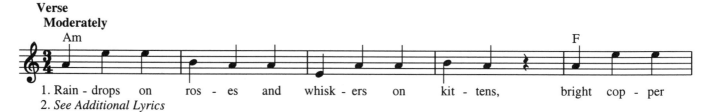

1. Rain - drops on ros - es and whisk - ers on kit - tens, bright cop - per
2. *See Additional Lyrics*

ket - tles and warm wool - en mit - tens, brown pa - per pack - ag - es

tied up with strings, these are a few of my fa - vor - ite things.

fa - vor - ite things. When the dog bites, when the

bee stings, when I'm feel - ing sad, _____ I

sim - ply re - mem - ber my fa - vor - ite things and then I don't

feel _____ so bad. _____

Additional Lyrics

2. Cream colored ponies and crisp apple strudels,
   Doorbells and sleighbells and schnitzel with noodles,
   Wild geese that fly with the moon on their wings,
   These are a few of my favorite things.

No Particular Place to Go

Words and Music by Chuck Berry

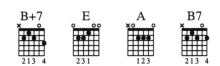

Strum Pattern: 1
Pick Pattern: 2

1. Rid - ing a - long in my au - to - mo - bile,
2., 3., 4. See Additional Lyrics

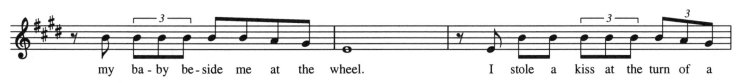

my ba - by be - side me at the wheel. I stole a kiss at the turn of a

mile, my cu - ri - os - i - ty run - ning wild.

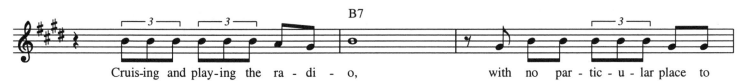

Cruis - ing and play - ing the ra - di - o, with no par - tic - u - lar place to

go. 2. Rid - ing a - long in my au - to - mo - go. ___

Additional Lyrics

2. Riding along in my automobile,
   I was anxious to tell her the way I feel.
   So I told her softly and sincere
   And she leaned and whispered in my ear.
   Cuddling more and driving slow,
   With no particular place to go.

3. No particular place to go,
   So we parked way out on the cocamo.
   The night was young and the moon was gold,
   So we both decided to take a stroll.
   Can you image the way I felt?
   I couldn't unfasten her safety belt.

4. Riding along in my calaboose,
   Still trying to get her belt unloose.
   All the way home I held a grudge,
   For the safety belt that wouldn't budge.
   Crusing and playing the radio,
   With no particular place to go.

Papa Loved Mama

Words and Music by Kim Williams and Garth Brooks

Strum Pattern: 2
Pick Pattern: 4

Verse
Driving Beat

1. Pa - pa drove a truck near - ly all his life. You know it
2. *See Additional Lyrics*

drove Ma - ma cra - zy be - ing a truck - er's wife. The part she could-n't han - dle was the

be - ing a - lone. __ I guess she need - ed more to hold than just a tel - e - phone. ___ Pa-

- pa called Ma - ma each and ev - 'ry night just to ask ___ her how she was and if us

kids were al - right. Ma - ma would wait ___ for that call ___ to come in ___ but when Dad-

- dy'd hang up she was gone a - gain. ___ Ma-

See Additional Lyrics

Additional Lyrics

2. Well, it was bound to happen and one night it did.
   Papa came home and it was just us kids.
   He had a dozen roses and a bottle of wine.
   If he was lookin' to surprise us he was doin' fine.
   I heard him cry for Mama up and down the hall.
   Then I heard a bottle break against the bedroom wall.
   That old diesel engine made an eerie sound,
   When Papa fired it up and headed into town.

Chorus Oh, the picture in the paper showed the scene real well.
   Papa's rig was buried in the local motel.
   The desk clerk said he saw it all real clear.
   He never hit the brakes and he was shifting gears.

Rhiannon

Words and Music by Stevie Nicks

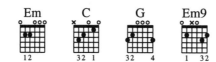

Em   C   G   Em9

Strum Pattern: 1
Pick Pattern: 2

Intro
Moderately

1. Rhi -

Verse

an - non rings __ like a bell thru the night, and would-n't you love to love __ her? __
2. *See Additional Lyrics*

Takes to the sky like a bird in flight __ and who will be __ her lov - er?

Bridge

All your life __ you've nev - er seen a wom-an __ tak - en by the wind. __

Would you stay __ if she prom - ised you heav - en? Will you ev - er win? _____

Chorus

Will you ev - er win? _____   Rhi - an - non.

Outro   *Repeat and Fade*

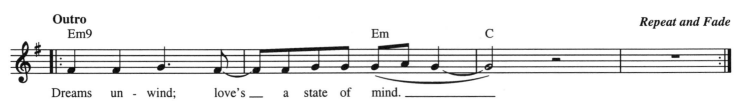

Dreams un - wind; love's __ a state of mind. _____

Additional Lyrics

2. She is like a cat in the dark,
   And then she is the darkness.
   She rules her life like a fine skylark,
   And when the sky is starless.

Satin Doll

from SOPHISTICATED LADIES
Words by Johnny Mercer and Billy Strayhorn
Music by Duke Ellington

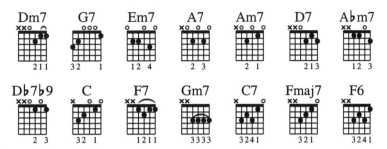

Strum Pattern: 4
Pick Pattern: 1

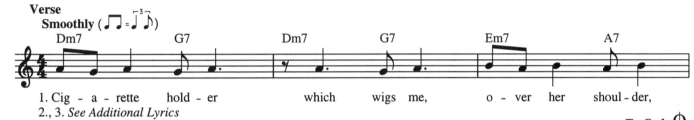

1. Cig - a - rette hold - er which wigs me, o - ver her shoul - der,
2., 3. *See Additional Lyrics*

she digs me. Out cat - tin' that sat - in doll.

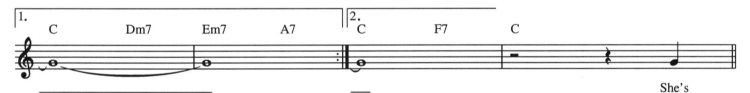

She's

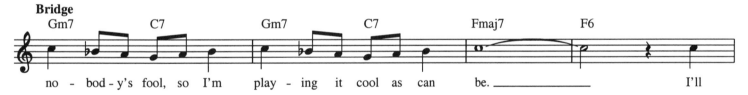

no - bod - y's fool, so I'm play - ing it cool as can be. I'll

give it a whirl, but I ain't for no girl catch - ing me.

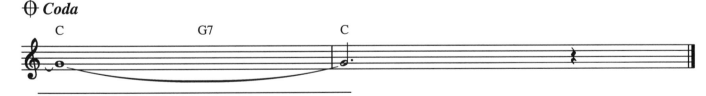

Additional Lyrics

2. Baby shall we go out skippin'?
   Careful amigo, you're flippin'.
   Speaks Latin, that satin doll.

3. Telephone numbers well you know,
   Doin' my rhumbas with uno,
   And that 'n' my satin doll.

Silent Night

Words by Joseph Mohr
Music by Franz Gruber

Strum Pattern: 7
Pick Pattern: 9

Verse
Quietly

1. Si - lent night, ho - ly night! All is calm,
2., 3. *See Additional Lyrics*

all is bright. Round yon Vir - gin Moth - er and Child.

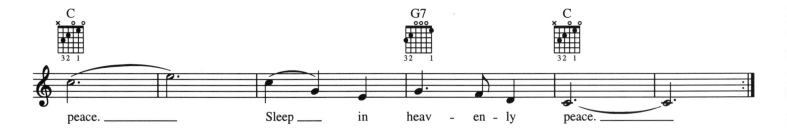

Ho - ly In - fant so ten - der and mild, sleep in heav - en - ly

peace. _____ Sleep ___ in heav - en - ly peace. _____

Additional Lyrics

2. Silent night, holy night!
   Shepherds quake at the sight.
   Glories stream from heaven afar.
   Heavenly hosts sing Alleluia.
   Christ the Savior is born!
   Christ the Savior is born!

3. Silent night, holy night!
   Son of God, love's pure light.
   Radiant beams from thy holy face
   With the dawn of redeeming grace,
   Jesus Lord at Thy birth.
   Jesus Lord at Thy birth.

Stormy Weather
(Keeps Rainin' All the Time)

from COTTON CLUB PARADE OF 1933
Lyric by Ted Koehler
Music by Harold Arlen

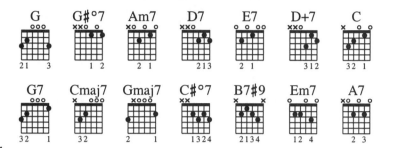

Strum Pattern: 4
Pick Pattern: 4

Additional Lyrics

2. Life is bare, gloom and mis'ry ev'rywhere.
   Stormy weather, just can't get my poor self together.
   I'm weary all the time, the time,
   So weary all the time.

3. Can't go on, ev'rything I had is gone.
   Stormy weather, since my { man / gal } and I ain't together,
   Keeps rainin' all the time,
   Keeps rainin' all the time.

This Old Man

Traditional

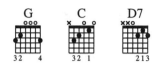

Strum Pattern: 3
Pick Pattern: 3

Verse
Lively

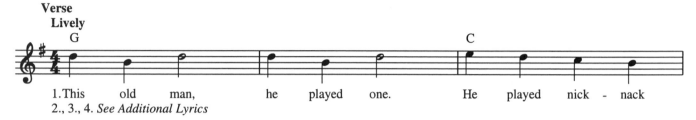

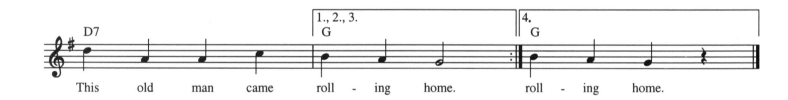

1. This old man, he played one. He played nick-nack
2., 3., 4. *See Additional Lyrics*

on my drum with a nick-nack pad-dy whack, give your dog a bone.

This old man came roll-ing home. roll-ing home.

Additional Lyrics

2. This old man, he played two.
   He played nicknack on my shoe with a
   Nicknack paddy whack, give your dog a bone.
   This old man came rolling home.

3. This old man, he played three.
   He played nicknack on my knee with a
   Nicknack paddy whack, give your dog a bone.
   This old man came rolling home.

4. This old man, he played four.
   He played nicknack on my door with a
   Nicknack paddy whack, give your dog a bone.
   This old man came rolling home.

Ticket to Ride

Words and Music by John Lennon and Paul McCartney

Strum Pattern: 4
Pick Pattern: 1

Additional Lyrics

2., 4. She said that livin' with me is bringin' her down, yeah.
For she would never be free when I was around.

Three Times a Lady

Words and Music by Lionel Richie

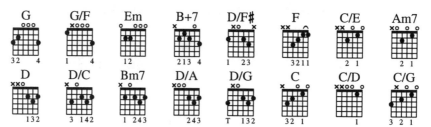

Strum Pattern: 8
Pick Pattern: 8

Verse
Slowly

Thanks for the times that you've giv - en me. ___ The

mem - 'ries ___ are all ___ in my mind. ___ And

now that we've come to the end of our rain - bow,

there's some - thing ___ I must ___ say out ___ loud. ___

Chorus

You're once, twice, three times ___
a ___ la - dy, ___ and I love ___ you. ___

Yes, you're once, twice,

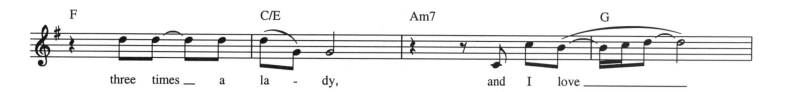

three times — a la - dy, and I love _____

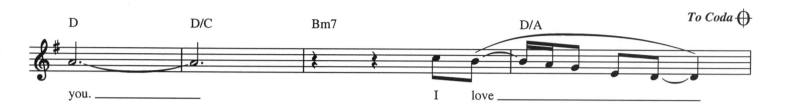

To Coda ⊕

you. _____ I love _____

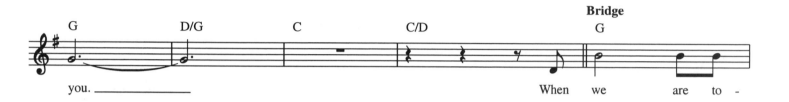

Bridge

you. _____ When we are to -

geth - er, _____ the mo - ments I cher - ish _____ with ev - 'ry beat _____

_____ of my _____ heart. _____ To touch you, _____ to

hold you, _____ to feel you, _____ to need you, _____ there's noth - ing _____ to

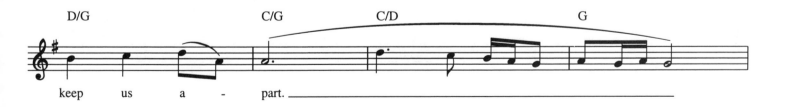

keep us a - part. _____

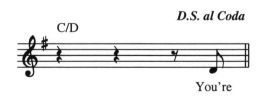

D.S. al Coda

You're

⊕ *Coda*

you.

True Love

from HIGH SOCIETY

Words and Music by Cole Porter

Tulsa Time

Words and Music by Danny Flowers

Strum Pattern: 1
Pick Pattern: 1

Verse
Moderate Boogie

Additional Lyrics

2. Well, there I was in Hollywood,
   Wishin' I was doing good,
   Talkin' on the telephone line.
   But they don't need me in the movies
   And nobody sings my songs,
   Guess I'm just a wastin' time.
   Well, then I got to thinkin',
   Man, I'm really sinkin'
   And I really had a flash this time.
   I had no bus'ness leavin' and nobody would be grievin'
   If I went on back to Tulsa time.

Chorus 2 Livin' on Tulsa time.
   Livin' on Tulsa time.
   Gonna set my watch back to it,
   'Cause you know I've been through it,
   Livin' on Tulsa time.

Unchained Melody

from the Motion Picture UNCHAINED
Lyric by Hy Zaret
Music by Alex North

Additional Lyrics

Bridge Lonely mountains gaze
At the stars, at the stars,
Waiting for the dawn of the day.
All alone, I gaze
At the stars, at the stars,
Dreaming of my love far away.

When I Fall in Love

Words by Edward Heyman
Music by Victor Young

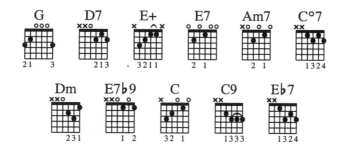

Strum Pattern: 1, 3
Pick Pattern: 2, 3

Slowly

When I fall in love it will be for-ev-er, or I'll nev-er

fall in love. _____ In a rest-less world like this is, love is

end-ed be-fore it's be-gun, and too man-y moon-light kiss-es seem to

cool in the warmth of the sun. When I give my heart it will be com-

plete-ly, or I'll nev-er give my heart; _____ And the

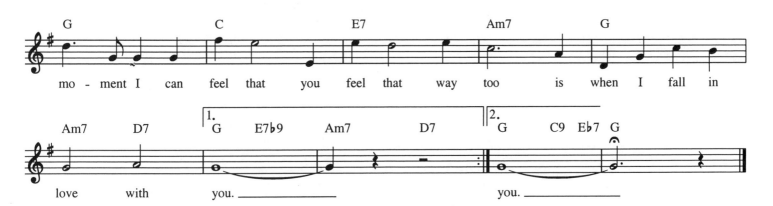

mo-ment I can feel that you feel that way too is when I fall in

love with you. _____   you. _____

Will the Circle Be Unbroken

Words and Music by Eddy Arnold

Strum Pattern: 2
Pick Pattern: 2

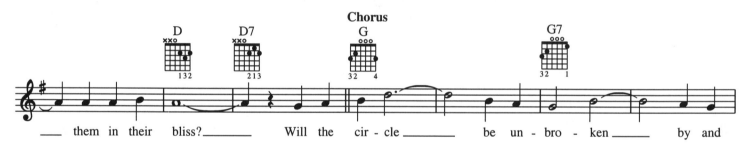

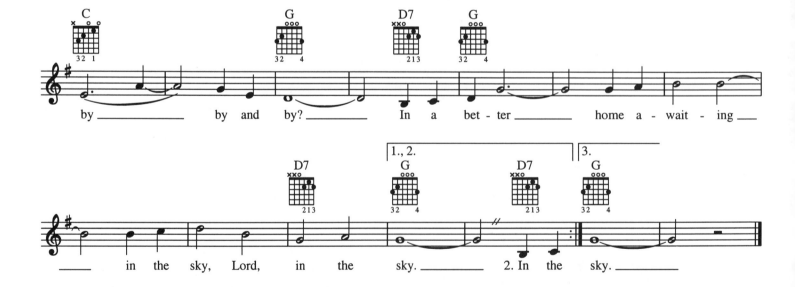

Additional Lyrics

2. In the joyous days of childhood oft' they told of wond'rous love.
   Pointed to the dying Savior, now they dwell with Him above.

3. You can picture happy gath'rings 'round the fireside long ago.
   And you think of tearful partings when they left you here below.

Yesterday

Words and Music by John Lennon and Paul McCartney

Strum Pattern: 1, 3
Pick Pattern: 2, 4

Verse
Moderately Slow

1. Yes - ter - day all my trou - bles seemed so far a - way,
2. *See Additional Lyrics*

now it looks as though they're here to stay. _ Oh, I be - lieve _ in yes - ter - day. _

Bridge

Why she had to go I don't know, she would - n't say.

I said some - thing wrong, now I long for yes - ter - day.

Verse

3., 4. Yes - ter - day love was such an eas - y game to play, _

now I need a place to hide a - way. _ Oh, I be - lieve _ in

1. yes - ter - day. _
2. yes - ter - day. Mm. _

Additional Lyrics

2. Suddenly, I'm not half the man I used to be.
There's a shadow hanging over me.
Oh, yesterday came suddenly.

You Give Love a Bad Name

Words and Music by Jon Bon Jovi, Richie Sambora and Desmond Child

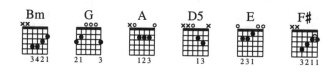

Strum Pattern: 4
Pick Pattern: 3

Intro
Moderate Rock

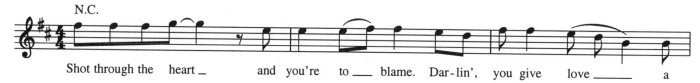

Shot through the heart _ and you're to _ blame. Dar-lin', you give love _ a

bad name.

Verse

1. An an-gel's smile _ is what you sell. You
2. *See Additional Lyrics*

prom - ise me heav - en, then put me through hell. Chains of _ love _ got a

hold on me. When pas - sion's a pris - on, you can't break _ free.

Pre-Chorus

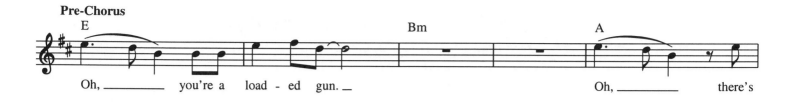

Oh, _____ you're a load-ed gun. _____ Oh, _____ there's

no-where to run, no one can save me, the dam-age is done.

Chorus

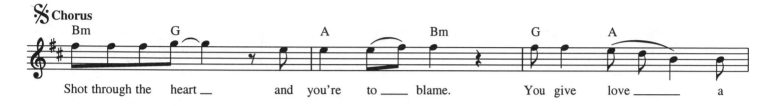

Shot through the heart _____ and you're to _____ blame. You give love _____ a

bad name. (Bad name.) I play my part _____ and you play your _ game. You give love _____ a

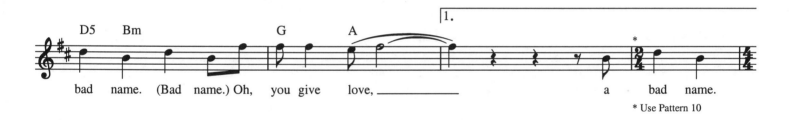

bad name. (Bad name.) Oh, you give love, _____ a bad name.

* Use Pattern 10

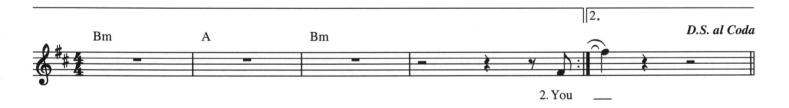

2. You _____

Coda **Outro** *Repeat and Fade*

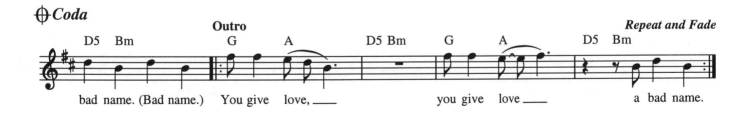

bad name. (Bad name.) You give love, _____ you give love _____ a bad name.

Additional Lyrics

2. You paint your smile on your lips.
   Blood-red nails on your fingertips.
   A schoolboy's dream, you act so shy.
   Your very first kiss was your first kiss goodbye.

Autumn in New York

Words and Music by Vernon Duke

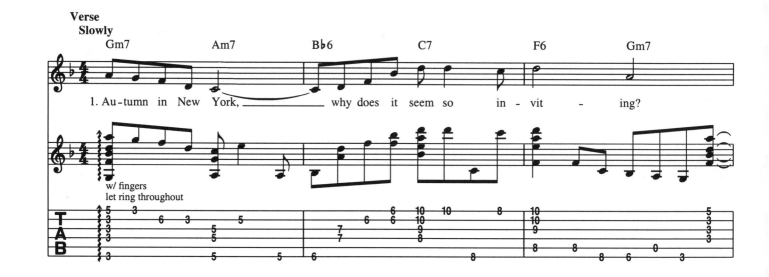

shim-mer - ing clouds in can-yons of steel, _____ they're

mak - ing me feel _____ I'm home. _____

2. It's aut-umn in New York, _____ that brings the prom-ise of

new love; au-tumn in New York. _____

Georgia on My Mind

Words by Stuart Gorrell
Music by Hoagy Carmichael

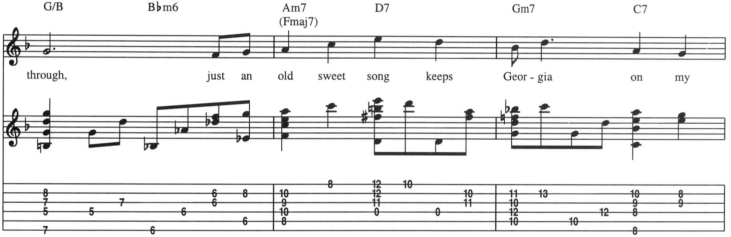

The Girl from Ipanema
(Garôta de Ipanema)

English Words by Norman Gimbel
Original Words by Vinicius de Moraes
Music by Antonio Carlos Jobim

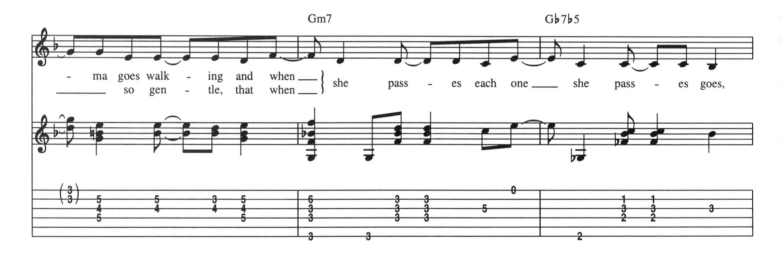

Isn't It Romantic?

from the Paramount Picture LOVE ME TONIGHT

Words by Lorenz Hart
Music by Richard Rodgers

Alman

By Robert Johnson

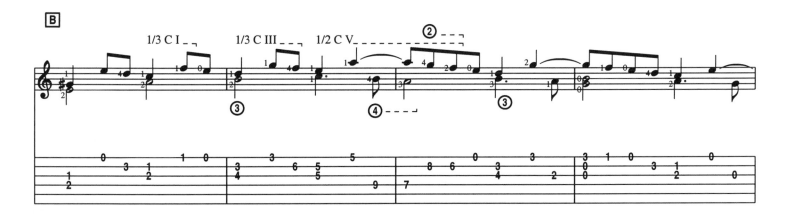

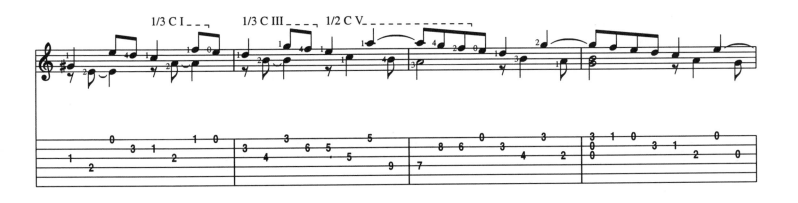

Bourrée

from LUTE SUITE NO. 1

By Johann Sebastian Bach

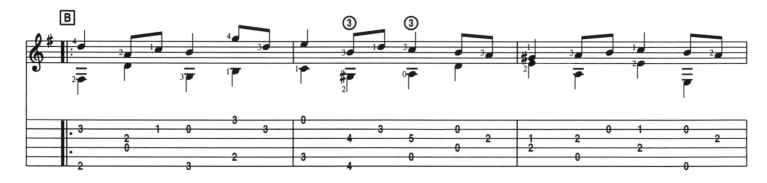

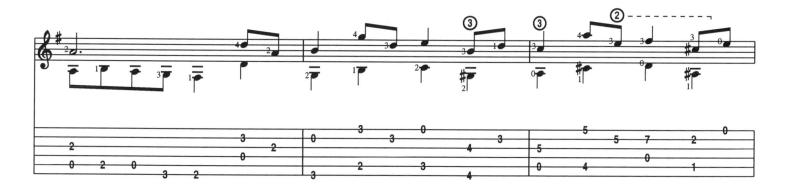

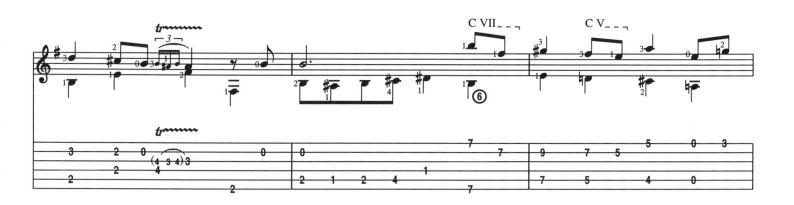

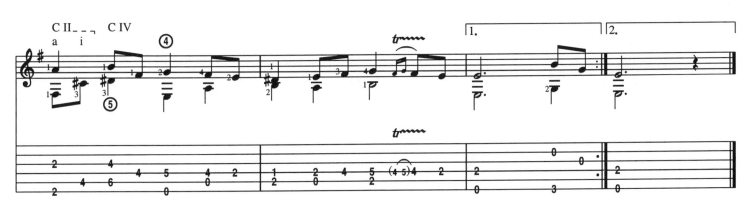

Estudio

By Francisco Tarrega

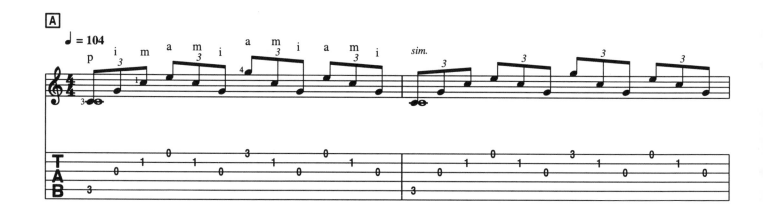

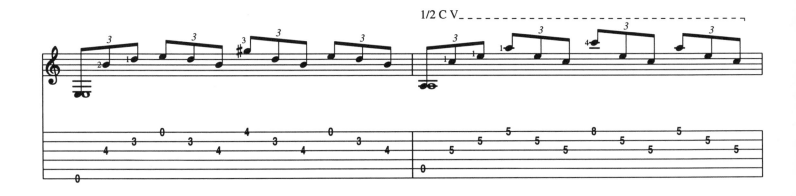

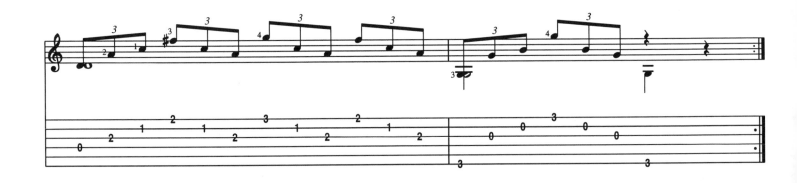

March

By Fernando Sor

crescendo poco a poco

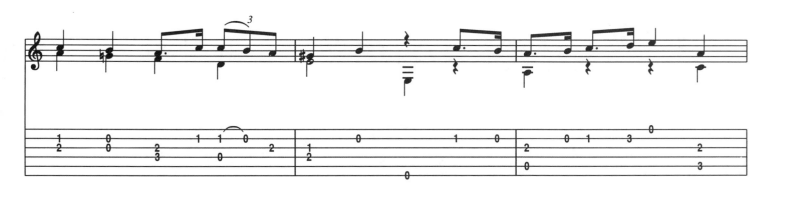

Study in A Minor

(Op. 60, No. 7)

By Matteo Carcassi

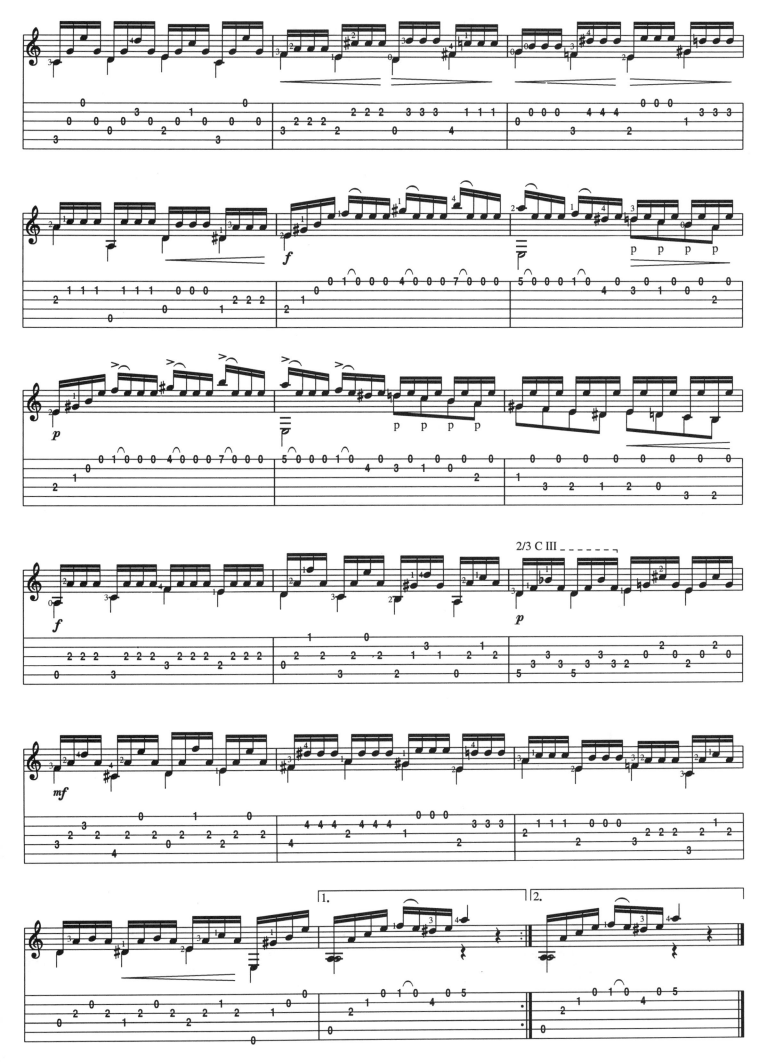

Españoleta

By Gaspar Sanz

Amazing Grace

Words by John Newton
Traditional American Melody

Drop D Tuning:
①=E ④=D
②=B ⑤=A
③=G ⑥=D

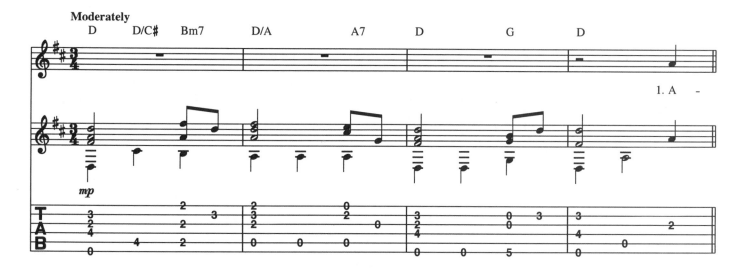

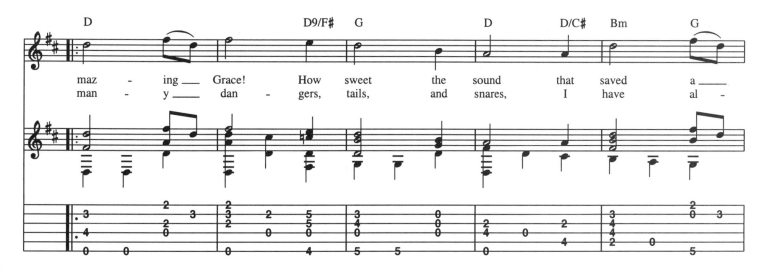

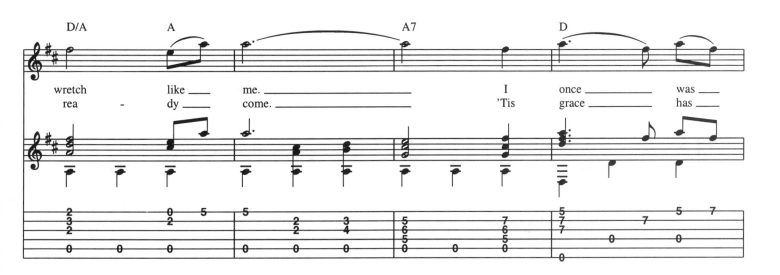

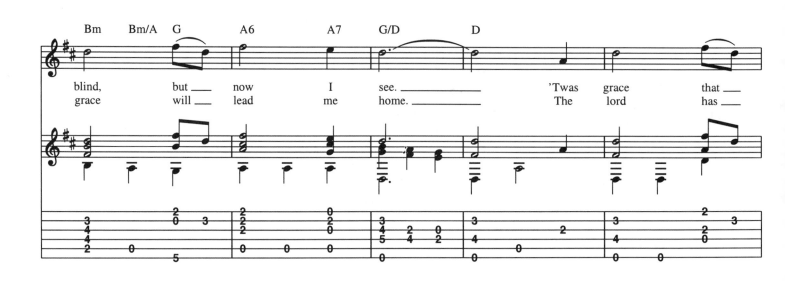

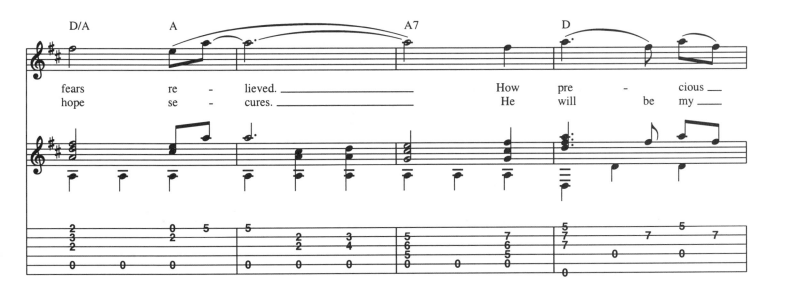

fears re - lieved. _____ How pre - cious ____
hope se - cures. _____ He will be my ____

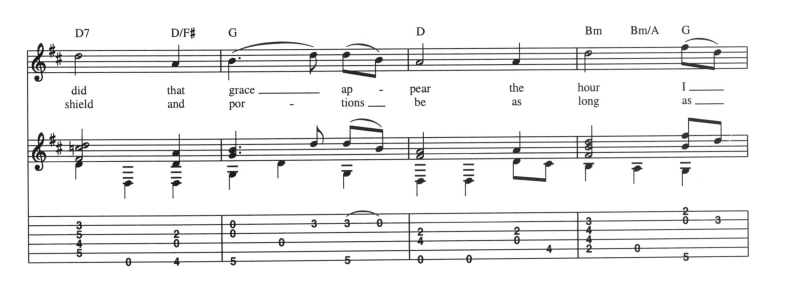

did that grace ____ ap - pear the hour I ____
shield and grace por - tions ____ be as long as ____

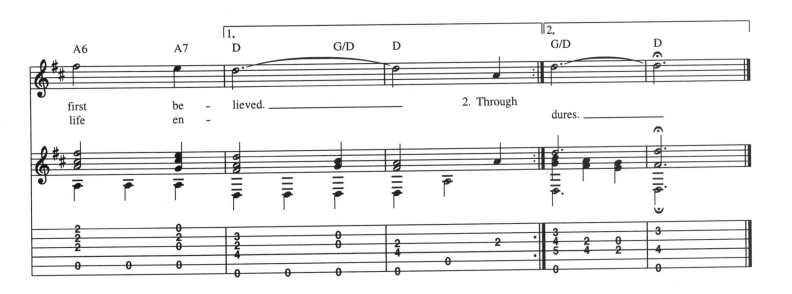

first be - lieved. _____ 2. Through
life en - dures. _____ dures. _____

Autumn Leaves
(Les Feuilles Mortes)

English lyric by Johnny Mercer
French lyric by Jacques Prevert
Music by Joseph Kosma

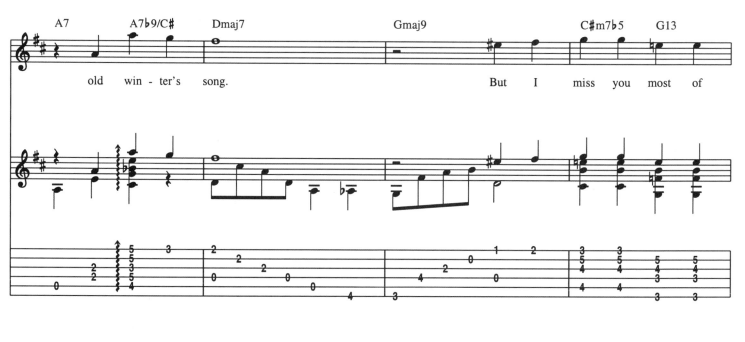

old win - ter's song. But I miss you most of

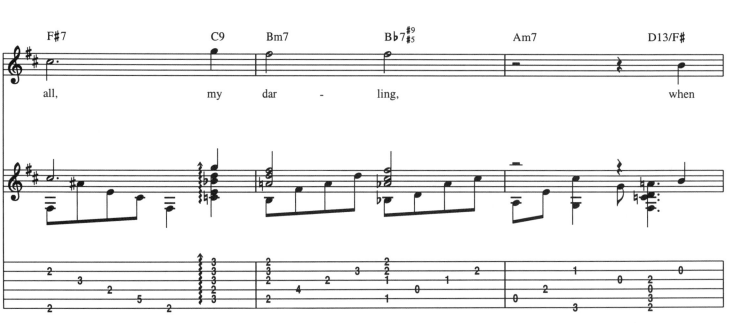

all, my dar - ling, when

au - tumn leaves start to fall.

My Heart Will Go On

(Love Theme From 'Titanic')
from the Paramount and Twentieth Century Fox Motion Picture TITANIC

Music by James Horner
Lyric by Will Jennings

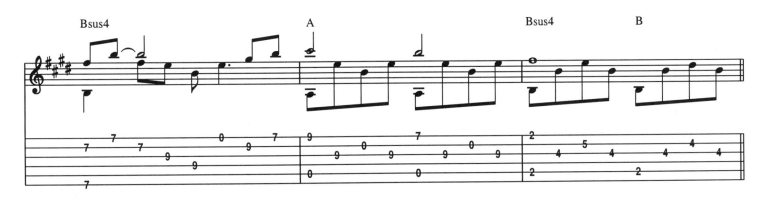

and you're here   in my   heart, and   my   heart will   go

To Coda ⊕ **Interlude**

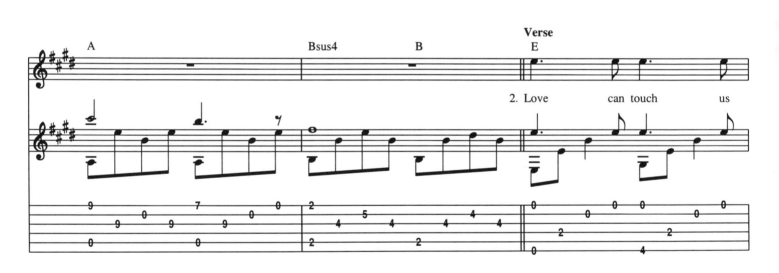

on   and   on.

Verse

2. Love   can touch   us

one   time   and   last for   a   life -   time,

224

Greensleeves

Traditional

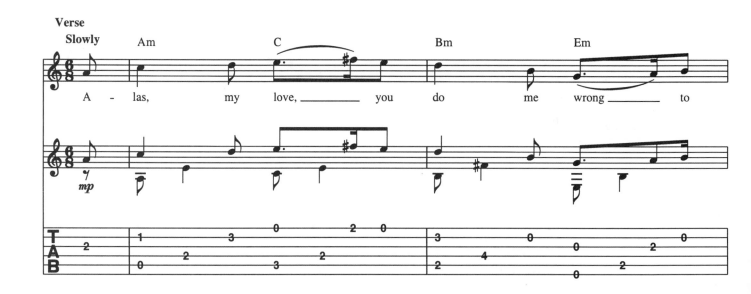

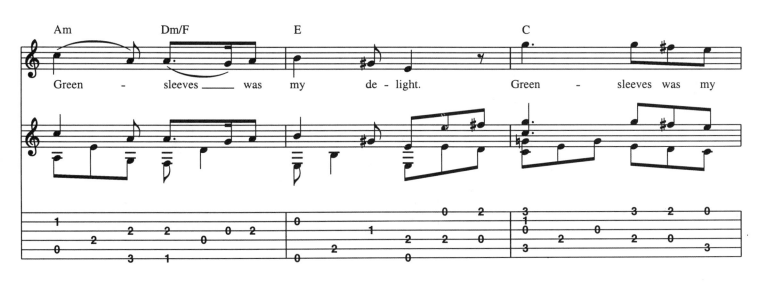

Wonderful Tonight

Words and Music by Eric Clapton

1. It's late in the even - ing; she's won-d'ring what clothes to wear.
2. We go to a par - ty and ev - 'ry - one turns to see
3. It's time to go home now, and I've got an ach - ing head.

She puts on her make - up and brush-es her long blond hair.
this beau - ti - ful la - dy is walk-ing a - round with me.
So I give her the car keys, and she helps me to bed.

229

Angie

Words and Music by Mick Jagger and Keith Richards

Intro

Slowly ♩ = 73

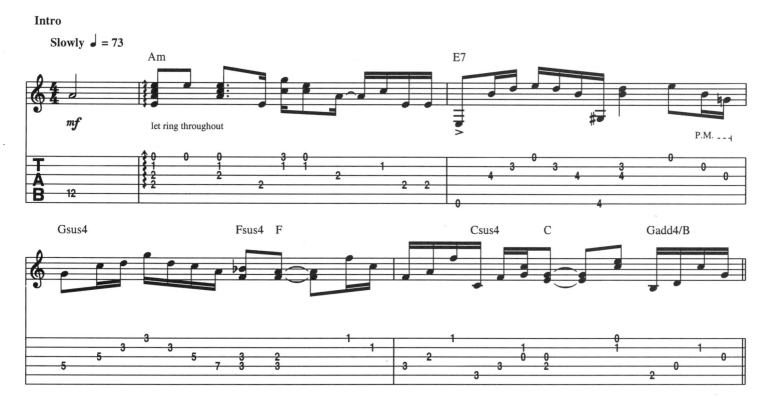

Babe, I'm Gonna Leave You

Words and Music by Anne Bredon, Jimmy Page and Robert Plant

Intro

Moderately ♩ = 134

*T = Thumb on ⑥

Born to Be Wild
Words and Music by Mars Bonfire

Brown Eyed Girl
Words and Music by Van Morrison

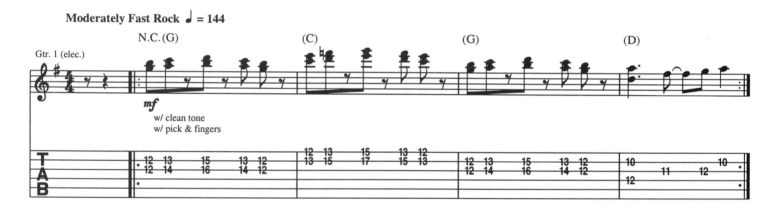

Don't Fear the Reaper
Words and Music by Donald Roeser

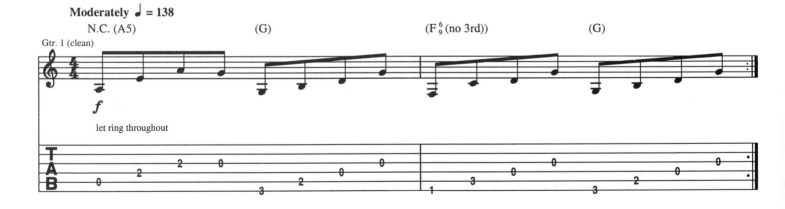

Dust in the Wind

Words and Music by Kerry Livgren

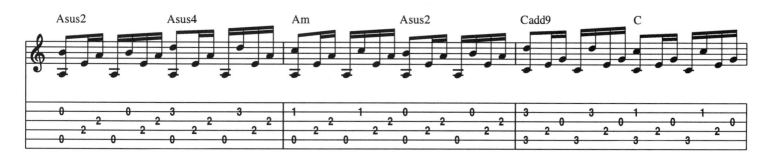

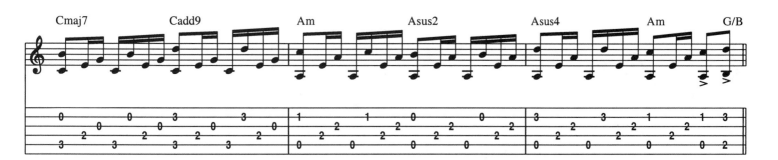

Gimmie Three Steps

Words and Music by Allen Collins and Ronnie Van Zant

Here Comes the Sun
Words and Music by George Harrison

Capo VII

Intro

Moderately Uptempo ♩ = 144

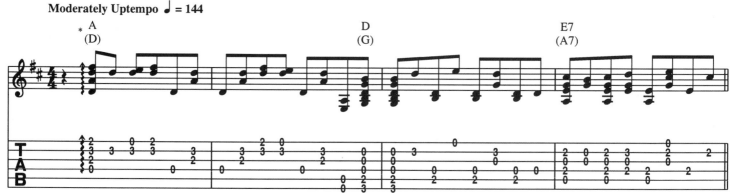

* Symbols in parentheses represent chord names respective to capoed guitar.
Symbols above reflect actual sounding chord. Capoed fret is "O" in TAB.

Layla
Words and Music by Eric Clapton and Jim Gordon

Moderately ♩ = 116

Love Song

Words and Music by Jeffrey Keith and Frank Hannon

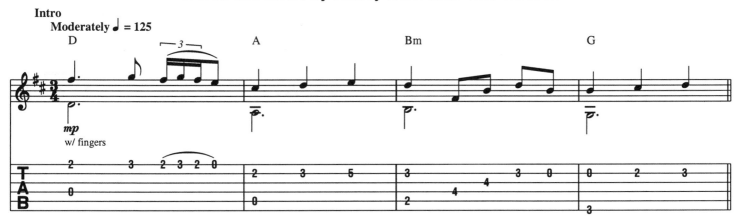

My Girl

Words and Music by William "Smokey" Robinson and Ronald White

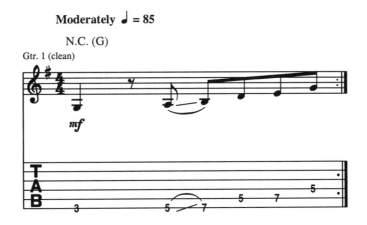

Paranoid

**Words and Music by Anthony Iommi, John Osbourne,
William Ward and Terence Butler**

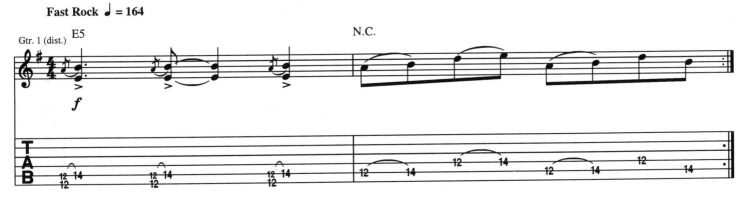

Pride and Joy
Written by Stevie Ray Vaughan

Tune Down 1/2 Step:

① = Eb ④ = Db
② = Bb ⑤ = Ab
③ = Gb ⑥ = Eb

Medium Shuffle ♩ = 122

Rock and Roll All Nite
Words and Music by Paul Stanley and Gene Simmons

Anthem Rock ♩ = 156

School's Out
Words and Music by Alice Cooper, Neal Smith, Michael Bruce, Glen Buxton and Dennis Dunaway

Moderate Rock ♩ = 132

Silent Lucidity

Words and Music by Chris DeGarmo

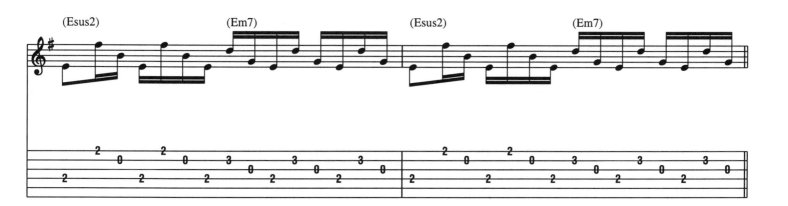

Susie-Q

Words and Music by Dale Hawkins, Stan Lewis and Eleanor Broadwater

Takin' Care of Business
Words and Music by Randy Bachman

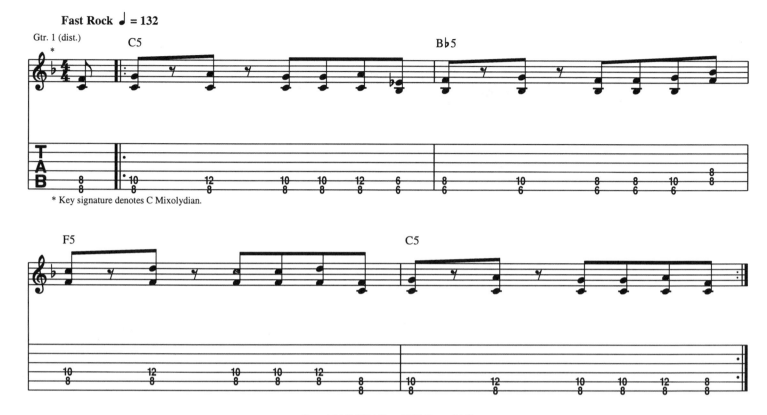

* Key signature denotes C Mixolydian.

Tears in Heaven
Words and Music by Eric Clapton and Will Jennings

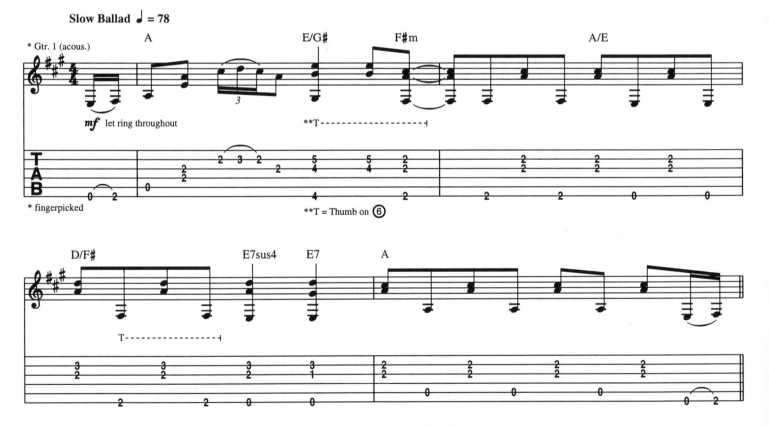

STRUM AND PICK PATTERNS

This chart contains the suggested strum and pick patterns that are referred to by number at the beginning of each song in this book. The symbols ⊓ and ∨ in the strum patterns refer to down and up strokes, respectively. The letters in the pick patterns indicate which right-hand fingers plays which strings.

p = thumb
i = index finger
m = middle finger
a = ring finger

For example; Pick Pattern 2
is played: thumb - index - middle - ring

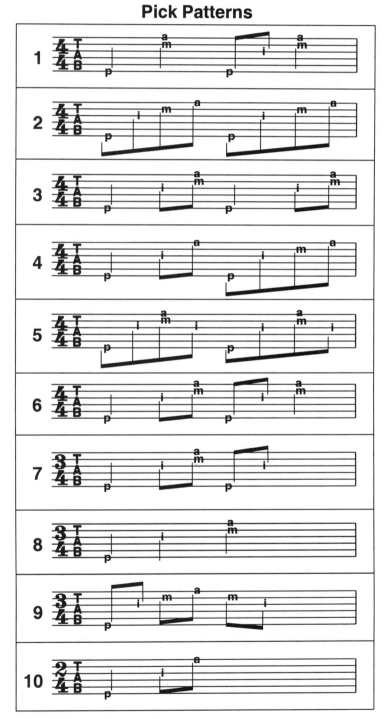

You can use the 3/4 Strum or Pick Patterns in songs written in compound meter (6/8, 9/8, 12/8, etc.).
For example, you can accompany a song in 6/8 by playing the 3/4 pattern twice in each measure.
The 4/4 Strum and Pick Patterns can be used for songs written in cut time (¢) by doubling the note time values in the patterns. Each pattern would therefore last two measures in cut time.

Guitar Notation Legend

Guitar Music can be notated three different ways: on a *musical staff*, in *tablature*, and in *rhythm slashes*.

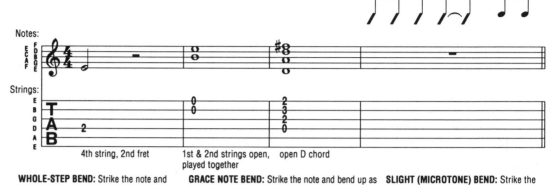

RHYTHM SLASHES are written above the staff. Strum chords in the rhythm indicated. Use the chord diagrams found at the top of the first page of the transcription for the appropriate chord voicings. Round noteheads indicate single notes.

THE MUSICAL STAFF shows pitches and rhythms and is divided by bar lines into measures. Pitches are named after the first seven letters of the alphabet.

TABLATURE graphically represents the guitar fingerboard. Each horizontal line represents a string, and each number represents a fret.

4th string, 2nd fret   1st & 2nd strings open, played together   open D chord

HALF-STEP BEND: Strike the note and bend up 1/2 step.

WHOLE-STEP BEND: Strike the note and bend up one step.

GRACE NOTE BEND: Strike the note and bend up as indicated. The first note does not take up any time.

SLIGHT (MICROTONE) BEND: Strike the note and bend up 1/4 step.

BEND AND RELEASE: Strike the note and bend up as indicated, then release back to the original note. Only the first note is struck.

PRE-BEND: Bend the note as indicated, then strike it.

VIBRATO: The string is vibrated by rapidly bending and releasing the note with the fretting hand.

WIDE VIBRATO: The pitch is varied to a greater degree by vibrating with the fretting hand.

HAMMER-ON: Strike the first (lower) note with one finger, then sound the higher note (on the same string) with another finger by fretting it without picking.

PULL-OFF: Place both fingers on the notes to be sounded. Strike the first note and without picking, pull the finger off to sound the second (lower) note.

LEGATO SLIDE: Strike the first note and then slide the same fret-hand finger up or down to the second note. The second note is not struck.

SHIFT SLIDE: Same as legato slide, except the second note is struck.

TRILL: Very rapidly alternate between the notes indicated by continuously hammering on and pulling off.

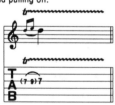

TAPPING: Hammer ("tap") the fret indicated with the pick-hand index or middle finger and pull off to the note fretted by the fret hand.

NATURAL HARMONIC: Strike the note while the fret-hand lightly touches the string directly over the fret indicated.

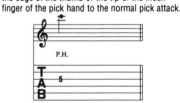

PINCH HARMONIC: The note is fretted normally and a harmonic is produced by adding the edge of the thumb or the tip of the index finger of the pick hand to the normal pick attack.

PICK SCRAPE: The edge of the pick is rubbed down (or up) the string, producing a scratchy sound.

MUFFLED STRINGS: A percussive sound is produced by laying the fret hand across the string(s) without depressing, and striking them with the pick hand.

PALM MUTING: The note is partially muted by the pick hand lightly touching the string(s) just before the bridge.

RAKE: Drag the pick across the strings indicated with a single motion.

TREMOLO PICKING: The note is picked as rapidly and continuously as possible.

VIBRATO BAR DIVE AND RETURN: The pitch of the note or chord is dropped a specified number of steps (in rhythm) then returned to the original pitch.

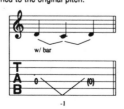

VIBRATO BAR SCOOP: Depress the bar just before striking the note, then quickly release the bar.

VIBRATO BAR DIP: Strike the note and then immediately drop a specified number of steps, then release back to the original pitch.